Abdul Karim Bangura
& Martin C. Muo

United States Congress & Bilingual Education

PETER LANG
New York • Washington, D.C./Baltimore • Bern
Frankfurt am Main • Berlin • Brussels • Vienna • Oxford

Library of Congress Cataloging-in-Publication Data

Bangura, Abdul Karim.
United States Congress and bilingual education /
Abdul Karim Bangura and Martin C. Muo.
p. cm.— (Independent volume)
1. Education, Bilingual— Government policy— United States. 2. Education,
Bilingual— Law and legislation— United States. 3. Education,
Bilingual— Political aspects— United States.
I. Muo, Martin C. II. Title. III. Series.
LC3731.B35   370.117'5'0973— DC21   98-9862
ISBN 0-8204-4000-0

Die Deutsche Bibliothek-CIP-Einheitsaufnahme

Bangura, Abdul Karim:
United States Congress and bilingual education /
Abdul Karim Bangura and Martin C. Muo.
–New York; Washington, D.C./Baltimore; Bern;
Frankfurt am Main; Berlin; Brussels; Vienna; Oxford: Lang.
ISBN 0-8204-4000-0

Cover design by Nona Reuter

The paper in this book meets the guidelines for permanence and durability
of the Committee on Production Guidelines for Book Longevity
of the Council of Library Resources.

∞

© 2001 Peter Lang Publishing, Inc., New York

Printed in the United States of America

To LEP and NEP Students!

Acknowledgments

We extend sincere gratitude to the many persons without whom the completion of this book would have been impossible. Especially, we thank the readers of our earlier drafts of this manuscript: Babalola Cole, Alvin Thornton, Maurice Woodard, and Morris Levitt. We also extend our gratitude to our relatives and friends who patiently gave encouragement and displayed considerable forbearance during our preoccupation with this work.

Abdul Karim Bangura
Martin Chuks Muo
Washington, DC
July 1998

Contents

Preface

This book seeks to fill a gap in the literature of the politics of bilingual education in the United States: the role of the legislature in the passage of the 1968 Bilingual Education Act and its aftermath. In order to do so, four major questions are examined: (1) In what types of political, economic, social, and cultural environments did the debate on bilingual education emerge? (2) What are the positions of the competing factions that lobbied Congress on the issue of bilingual education, and how can they be characterized? (3) What shaped the roles played by the legislative branch in transforming inputs into outputs? (4) What are the outputs of the transformational processes, and how can they be characterized?

Employing a case study approach augmented by a slightly modified version of David Easton's "framework for political analysis" (by focusing on the American legislative branch), the data for examining these questions were collected from primary sources (face-to-face interviews and Congressional Records) and secondary sources (books, journal articles, newspaper articles, and magazine articles).

The substantive findings generated after the data analysis make it possible to delineate the following conclusions: (1) The 1964 election was crucial in getting Congress to pass the Act; (2) President Lyndon Johnson's ideology and style were important in shaping the type of environment conducive to the passage of the Act; (3) the time of the Act was opportune; (4) the major thorn in the bilingual education program was and still remains that of administration; (5) although initially conceived as an enrichment program, the Act had to be recast into a compensatory education program by the time it was signed into law; and (6) education policy in the United States has become increasingly politicized because of the language issue.

Chapter 1

INTRODUCTION

This book explores the politics of bilingual education, more specifically, the role of the legislature in the passage of the 1968 Bilingual Education Act and its aftermath. The importance of such a book was captured by Paulston when she noted the following:

> Who stands to gain, where 'gain' can be operationalized as an indicator of which group benefits in the power struggle. The literature on bilingual education is noticeable for the almost complete absence of such questions. The pious assumption is of course that the children are the ones who stand to gain, with indicators like standardized test scores on school achievement and self-concept (1974:57).

The preceding excerpt supports the need for a major examination of the political environment, inputs, and the legislative processes that led to the passage of the 1968 Bilingual Education Act and subsequent developments since its passage. Such an effort will make it possible to identify which groups have gained and/or stand to gain from bilingual education policy decisions.

A Brief Historical Background

The 1968 Bilingual Education Act or Title VII of the Elementary and Secondary Education Act of 1965, as amended, provided supplemental funding for school districts interested in establishing programs to meet the special educational needs of large numbers of children of limited English-speaking ability in the United States (20 USC §880b et seq, 1970). The children served under Title VII also had to be from low-income families (20

USC §880b–2a, 1970). Funding was provided for planning and developing bilingual programs, preservice training, and for operation of programs, including bilingual education, early childhood education, adult education, dropout programs, vocational programs, and courses dealing with the history and culture of the language minority group being served (20 USC §880b–2, 1970).

At the initiative of Congress, in response to demands, pressures, and inputs, particularly from delegates representing the states of California, Texas, and Florida, a program to improve the education of children of language minority groups was authorized in 1967. (Language minority groups refer to children who come from environments where the dominant language is other than English.) About three million children of school age were expected to benefit from these special programs funded under Title VII of the Bilingual Education Act of 1968. Although the focus was mostly on children of Mexican and Puerto Rican backgrounds, the initial response to the Act produced projects in 17 different languages.

The intention of Congress was obviously to satisfy the social, political, economic, and cultural environment with the passage of the 1968 Bilingual Education Act. However, like most laws, the 1968 Act had its problems. The major flaw was its failure to provide a systematic means of determining the success of programs funded under this Act. Thus, six years after the Act was passed, it was difficult, if not impossible, to determine how successful the programs were or what progress had been made to overcome the obstacles faced by language minority schoolchildren in the United States. This problem was later addressed by the Bilingual Education Act of 1974. This Act, which was more explicit in intent and design, eliminated the low-income criteria of the previous Act (the 1968 Bilingual Education Act) and provided a definition of what constitutes a bilingual education program. In the 1974 Act, Congress described bilingual education programs as those in which

> ...Instruction given in, and the study of, English and to the extent necessary to allow a child to progress effectively through the educational system the native language of the children of limited English-speaking ability, and such instruction is given with appreciation for the cultural heritage of such children, and, with respect to elementary school instruction, such instruction shall, to the extent necessary, be in all courses or subjects of study which will allow a child to progress effectively through the educational system (20 USC §800b–1 [a] [4] [A] [6], Supplement 1975).

Finally, the 1974 Act required the Commissioner of Education and the National Advisory Council for Bilingual Education (NACBE) to report to

Congress on the state of bilingual education in the United States. The Act thus mandated a continued assessment of the educational needs of the children of limited-English proficient (LEP) ability, thereby providing a feedback mechanism and progress report.

To further understand the politics of the 1968 Bilingual Education Act, it is important to explore the legislative process that put the said Act in place. Historically, education has been the responsibility of state and local governments in the United States. Federal involvement in educational policies was limited because of constitutional and jurisdictional prescriptions. The first major change in this regard came with the 1954 *Brown v Board of Education* (347 USC §483, 1954) desegregation decision by the United States Supreme Court. This landmark ruling opened and maintained federal intervention in educational policies which peaked in the 1960s with the 1964 Civil Rights Act (42 USC §2000d, 1970). This Act authorized the federal government to give technical and financial assistance to public schools in the process of segregation. Subsequently, the 1965 Elementary and Secondary Education Act, which provided federal aid for school districts with children of low-income families, was also passed. The 1965 Act was later amended, and thus, the 1968 Bilingual Education Act (the major focus of this book) emerged as a by-product of the Civil Rights movement of the 1960s.

The importance of equal opportunity to public education was underscored by the Supreme Court ruling in the case of *Brown v Board of Education*. Finding that segregated schools are inherently unequal, the Supreme Court held that State laws compelling black students to be educated separately from white students were unconstitutional. Following this decision in the 1960s were civil rights activities to end segregated schools. Much effort to overcome discrimination against language minority or non-English-speaking persons focused on schools. This approach was due to the fact that no public institution had a greater or more direct impact on the future of children than the schools.

In the case of bilingual education, the landmark case of *Lau v Nichols* (414 USC §563, 1974), which upheld the rights of non-English-speaking students to educational programs designed to meet their language-skill needs, became the cornerstone of the 1968 Bilingual Education Act. Later in 1974, the Supreme Court affirmed in *Lau* that school districts are compelled under Title VI of the Civil Rights Act of 1974 to provide children who speak little or no English with special language programs that will give them an equal opportunity to an education. Since then, proponents of bilingual education in both the academic and civil rights communities have based their arguments on Title VI, *Lau*, and the Equal Protection Clause of the Fourteenth Amendment to the Constitution of the United States.

With this brief historical background, this book focuses on the politics of the 1968 Bilingual Education Act, the role of Congress, and the aftermath of the legislation. The process and activities involved in the pursuit of legislation and its implementation for bilingual education are emphasized. Utilizing a slightly modified version of "systems" approach as set forth by David Easton in 1965 (because only the American legislative system is examined), this book analyzes the 1968 Bilingual Education Act by focusing on the United States Congress as the major unit of analysis.

The 1968 Bilingual Education Act: The Nature of the Problem

For almost two centuries, most Americans believed that language problems were foreign to their shores because of the assumption that everyone was learning and participating in wealth, power, and prestige through English (Kloss 1977). But, because of racial prejudice, some groups kept their differences, including language differences. The most well-known example of such segregation is, of course, the African American, who was obliged to learn varieties of English very quickly after arrival. In addition, the Japanese and Chinese, who crossed to the West Coast and Hawaii beginning in the nineteenth century, were kept out of the mainstream of American life. The largest groups are the Mexican Americans in the southwest and the Native Americans scattered throughout the country, each of whose settlements of North America preceded everyone else's. Because of their color and origin, these four groups have suffered years of discrimination and segregation, which have prevented them from participating fully in American society. Inevitably, most of their daily social and economic interactions have been with people who speak their languages; this is particularly true of Mexican Americans who, living close to Mexico, have also been in close touch with tens of millions of Spanish speakers. Spanish, Japanese, Chinese, and Native American languages have been useful to these segregated people, symbolizing the only identity allowed.

Greek, Polish, French, German, and Jewish Americans voluntarily pay for their children to learn elements of their ancestral tongues in weekend and full-day schools. Joshua Fishman estimated that there were about 600 private schools of which about one-fourth were full-day schools by 1980. In other words, these children did not attend public schools. All schools enrolled about 600,000 pupils (1980:107). While these schools nurtured ethnicity, their success in teaching languages was limited. As long as most Americans find that English is useful in the marketplace, promotion of other languages for communication within the United States faces an uphill battle.

Owing to the mass media and the educational system, even the most segregated communities have learned at least some English, and individuals from each group have become integrated into the wider society. However, several million poor Mexican Americans and Native Americans have dropped out of English language schools and have been left with minimal literacy in English. They were not literate in Spanish or Native American languages either, but they continued to speak and value them.

The antibilingual education groups, whose cause has been championed by United States English (USE), have made the following charges against the establishment of bilingual education during congressional hearings on the issue: (a) that there is no popular precedent for bilingual education; (b) that there is no historical precedent for bilingual education; (c) that most bilingual programs are geared toward the maintenance of the speakers' first language; (d) that young children will learn a second language in a very short period of time, so not much time is lost if they are placed in English-only classes; (e) that education in the native language takes away valuable time that could be spent on English; (f) that bilingual education is not effective; (g) that the number of eligible students is far smaller than estimated by probilingual education forces (for more on this, see Hakuta 1986:193-230).

There is research that bears on the preceding points, which the opponents of bilingual education frequently cite. For example, the American Institute for Research (AIR) concluded in 1978 that projects were improving students' Spanish-language competence without affecting their English ability, in contradiction to Congress' purpose (Hakuta 1986:230). Another observer, Malcolm Danoff (1978:10-14), warned that the programs may increase segregation of children according to language.

Supporters of bilingual education, on the other hand, have countered with a series of arguments during congressional hearings: (a) that bilingual schools existed in various parts of the country in the 19th century; (b) that bilingual education programs follow the policy of mainstreaming children into English-only classes as quickly as possible; (c) that public opinion surveys indicate considerable support for bilingual education as a method for language-minority students; (d) that children are not instantaneous second-language learners painted in our folklore, and it takes longer to learn the kinds of language skills necessary to perform well in school; (e) that there is considerable transfer of skills across languages, so that subject matter taught in one language does not have to be re-taught in the other; (f) that measures on effective issues used by the anti-bilingual education forces are flawed (see Hakuta 1986:196-230). Pro-bilingual education groups have also presented evidence showing increased intellectual development by children in bilingual education programs. In Montreal, Canada, for example, Wallace Lambert (1978) found that middle-class children who had studied in both French and English scored significantly higher than carefully matched monolinguals on both verbal and nonverbal measures of intelligence. Moreover, he added that they were also sure and confident in their identities.

These charges and their rebuttals led Congress to ask the Office of Bilingual Education (OBE) to evaluate bilingual education programs. But, the evaluations have been controversial and incomplete. Conflicting political and economic interests are at stake. No matter the results, someone will denounce them for alleged bias or dishonesty. This is mainly because a long-term commitment to the development of a weak language could mean a commitment of strengthening the political and economic base of its speakers separate from the larger community. If this happens to be the case, what measures must be taken to protect the interests of the whole? It can be suggested that bilingual education of Spanish-speakers in the American southwest, for example, will lead to a Quebec-like separatism. But starting with bilingual programs, aspiring political leaders might endeavor to build regional and ethnic loyalties in opposition to the larger community in order to promote their own careers.

In the 1960s, political leaders and educators decided to take action to abolish discrimination and lower the barriers to full participation. Their concern tended to focus on the approximately 10 million Mexican Americans and Native Americans. A new generation of leaders had come out of these two communities during the decade of the 1960s. Many had gone to universities in Texas and California or had moved to the cities of the midwest, where they gained a sense of their own identities and keen perception of the educational and economic problems facing Mexican Americans and Native Americans. Some ran for public office or started student, social, and labor movements which raised the consciousness of everyone about their plight (Garcia 1974). A new set of leaders and ideas also came from overseas. The post-World War II immigrations of intellectuals and professionals from Eastern Europe, the Mediterranean, and Asia awakened other Americans to the value of the languages and cultures of their ancestral homelands. They also heard about the worldwide resurgence of interest in ethnic identities. As a result of all these forces, a new generation of Americans expressed a desire to learn the languages abandoned by their immigrant grandparents and rejected by their parents.

Without the civil rights movement, however, calls for new policies concerning language could have been ignored. The Supreme Court decision in 1954 banning segregated schools opened a new chapter in American history. During the late 1950s and the 1960s, African American-led organizations pressed for changes in education, voting restrictions, housing restrictions, and discriminatory employment practices. The numerous laws passed, speeches by leaders of all races and religions, orders by Presidents John F. Kennedy, Lyndon B. Johnson, Richard M. Nixon, and Jimmy Carter, and the more than 400 African American officials elected to public office brought important changes in American society and finally affected the language issue. The Voting Rights Act of 1965, which ensured that African Americans in southern states would be able to participate through the ballot, also made it possible for Spanish-speaking Puerto Ricans living in New York state to vote.

Language legislation was given important support by President Johnson's "War on Poverty" in the mid-1960s. The President announced that the nation must embark upon a massive effort to raise income levels and reduce unemployment. Public opinion supported all these efforts to rid the country of misery and the remnants of racial discrimination and looked to the public schools as the major instrument of social change. Prior to 1960, America's public schools were almost exclusively supported by states, counties, and towns; but by the 1960s, Americans supported the idea that schools could play an increased role in social change. In response, Congress passed the Elementary and Secondary Education Act of 1965. New opportunities opened for all Americans as segregation and discrimination declined and as organized help to the poor began in a much more extensive way than ever before.

In this very favorable context, educators, Mexican Americans, and other community leaders urged Congress and the President to assist those Americans, who because of their inability to use English well, could not participate fully in American society. The relative poverty of Spanish speakers linked the call to action with other social programs. The new separatist message of the "black power" movement motivated some intellectuals and political leaders to speak and write about a need to recognize America as a culturally pluralistic society. This message led Senators and House members from California and Texas, two powerful states with significant Spanish-speaking populations, to sponsor and promote the bilingual education legislation (Judd 1977:62).

Taking all of the aforementioned factors into consideration, Congress responded by adding a "title" to the original 1965 Education Act. On January 2, 1968, the President signed Title VII or the Bilingual Education Act. Under this Act, Congress authorized $15 million for 1968, $39 million for 1969, and $40 million for 1970. This money was to be spent on the development of special education programs using English and the mother tongues of students. The money would also be spent on developing materials from the cultural backgrounds of Mexican Americans, Native Americans, and others that would be used in education. Provisions were also made for teacher training and some limited adult education.

Since 1968, Title VII has been amended. The most recent amendment passed on November 1, 1978, authorized the federal government to spend $200 million in 1979 with an increase of up to $400 million in 1983. Authorization by Congress does not necessarily mean that all of the money will be spent for bilingual education. Final appropriation depends on what projects are presented vis-à-vis other priorities. In practice, the sums actually spent have been increasing dramatically from $7.5 million in 1969 for 76 projects with 76,000 students to $158.6 million in 1979 for almost 600 projects using about 70 different languages. The number of students enrolled, primarily in elementary school programs, exceeded 300,000 in 1980. But, the proposed 1983 budget provided funds for only 125,000 children (NACBE 1979:6-11).

To administer the programs, Congress created the Office of Bilingual Education (OBE), a planning office within the Department of Education (DOE). The office suggests model programs, administers funds to set them up, and supervises studies designed to determine the extent of need for bilingual education programs. The Congress also created the National Advisory Council on Bilingual Education (NACBE), and most of its 15 members are educators from outside the government. The latter advises the director of OBE and prepares a comprehensive annual report on the state of bilingual education in order to improve models, develop teaching methods, and find ways to determine who needs such education.

With the election of Ronald Reagan as president in 1980, supporters of bilingual education realized that federal support was not enough to ensure adequate programs. They found that some programs might decline during his presidency. These supporters thus urged local and state governments, which have primary responsibility for public schools, to pass bilingual education laws. By 1980, 27 states had enacted such legislation either permitting or actually funding their own projects; 16 states still had no laws; and seven prohibited the use of any language other than English as the medium of instruction. Despite their laws, some cities in these seven states have received federal money for bilingual education. According to NACBE, only Alabama and Arkansas have had no schools engaged in bilingual instruction (NACBE 1979:11). This is due to the fact that these states did not have significant populations of NEP (non-English-proficient) or LEP students.

It is important to note that none of the laws providing funds for bilingual education require schools to use the various non-English languages. Many school districts have enthusiastically taken advantage of the opportunities for new programs, but others have not. It is the lower courts that have said that in certain circumstances schools must offer bilingual education. In the famous landmark case *Lau v Nichols* (414 USC §563, 1974), eighteen hundred Chinese-speaking native-born Americans in San Francisco claimed that the schools were denying them educational opportunity because they did not know English well. In January 1974, a unanimous Supreme Court declared that the school board would have to take remedial action because San Francisco was receiving federal funds for its schools and that the Civil Rights Act of 1964 had forbidden discrimination or the exclusion of anyone from a federally assisted program on the basis of "race, color, or national origin." The Chinese speakers were, the Court reasoned, excluded because of the language barrier that was related to their national origin—albeit indirect, since they were born in America. Although the high court did not specify a remedy, San Francisco chose to inaugurate a bilingual program. In the following months, the lower courts began to require a bilingual remedy in certain cases. In the case of *Serna v Portales Municipal Schools*, a circuit court declared that students who did not know English should receive bilingual instruction. In another case, *Aspira of New York*, a court also instructed schools to test the language proficiency of students to determine if they should be put into a bilingual program (CAL 1977:9–12).

By 1990, the DOE estimated that more than 3.5 million school-aged children were LEP learners. They could not follow lessons in English because their "test scores fall below the 40th percentile of a relevant comparison group," a rather vague criterion (DOE 1990:52053–52056). The Department proposed expanding and, for the first time, required bilingual programs to meet the needs of educating these children. In a series of proposed guidelines, the Department declared that schools receiving federal funds must determine the first language of its children and assess their skills in it. The education offered must then fit their language abilities. Those with poor English ability must receive some instruction in the mother tongue for at least two years. Congressional objections to the proposals prevented their implementation. Linguists also objected that national rules would undermine local initiatives and fail to take account of different groups' desires and needs. President Reagan effectively nullified the guidelines while indicating some skepticism about the whole bilingual education program (CAL 1977:1).

The Major Questions of This Book

As the preceding discussion clearly demonstrates, bilingual education, like many other issues that come before the legislature, has its staunch supporters and ardent opponents. Since one of the major objectives of this book is to examine the relationship between the role of the legislature and the push for a national bilingual education program, the major questions addressed here, in terms of a "systems" perspective, are the following:

1. In what types of political, economic, social, and cultural environments did the debate on bilingual education emerge?

2. What are the positions of the competing factions that lobbied Congress on the issue of bilingual education, and how can they be characterized?

3. What shaped the roles played by the legislative branch in transforming inputs into outputs?

4. What are the outputs of the transformational processes, and how can they be characterized?

While contemplating these questions, it is useful at this point to review the relevant works that have dealt with some aspects of bilingual education to ferret out the available suggestions. Because this book employs a political systems approach to examine the political struggle that led to the 1968 Bilingual Education Act and its aftermath, epistemological reasons call for the review of the available "political" literature on bilingual education, the literature on the legislature, and the literature on political systems theory. Studies on these topics are reviewed separately because of their different interests and foci. All three categories are also reviewed sequentially in order to trace their epistemological developments in a historical perspective.

Review of Relevant Works

Because most works on bilingualism in the United States concentrate on the linguistic and legal aspects of the issue, very little attention has been paid to the legislative processes that led to the passage of the 1968 Bilingual Education Act from a political science theory perspective. The few available works have also concentrated on the few themes that ignore the larger "power struggle" involved in the issue. The lack of works on the role of the legislature in bilingual education, as stated earlier, has been captured by Paulston. A review of the few available works on the topic, the major works on the legislative branch in its policy-making capacity, and the theoretical works on political systems analysis is presented.

Works on the Political Aspects of American Bilingualism

The works on the political aspects of bilingual education in America began with a focus on the role of politicians in introducing bilingual education bills (Stoller 1976). The focus then shifted to the ambition to make children functional bilinguals (Mackey and Beebe 1977). Litigation became the instrument for the spread of bilingual education (Teitelbaum and Hiller 1977, Birman and Ginsburg 1983). Chicano organizations in the southwest demanded equal opportunity programs, bilingual education (Blanco 1978), and a survey of the number of LEP students who received bilingual education after Title VII was enacted (O'Malley 1982). In sum, these studies concentrate their larger efforts on what Paulston has referred to as a "pervasive technocratic concern with methods, techniques, curriculum, and teacher training..." (1980:23).

This book is important, therefore, because it is couched within the premise that bilingual education can be well understood in terms of political conflicts. At stake are livelihoods, power, and prestige. In order to realize the value of this book, we must evaluate it in terms of the major works on the role of the legislature as policymaker and research on political systems analysis.

Works on the Legislature

The analysis of the role of the legislature in policy-making has attracted the attention of scholars for a long time. This interest in legislative studies has continued over time because of the nature and complexity of the functions of the legislature. These functions include policy formulation, legitimization, representation, and integration. Besides these functions, there are some enduring features that characterize the legislature in the United States. These characteristics, in part, constitute the basis for the analysis of the Act under study. An attempt is made to delineate the myths and general misconceptions about an Act of Congress. Eugene Eidenberg and Roy Morey note the following:

> Most of us think of an Act of Congress as being something permanent and final. But, if we look at Congressional acts over a period of time, we find that they rarely remain on the books in their original form. They are subsequently amended or replaced altogether. An Act of Congress represents a political decision made at one point in time. It may reflect the values of a majority in Congress at the time, though this is not always the case; it may also reflect the extent of knowledge regarding the issue at the time. Nevertheless, the act is not meant to be a once and for all resolution of a conflict. Most often the conflict continues inside or outside Congress and new laws are proposed which reshape the issue and ground rules reflecting new information (1969:175–176).

As one studies the role of the legislature in policy-making in general, and in the passage of the 1968 Bilingual Education Act in particular, these characteristic patterns become evident. However, due to the abundant nature of the literature on the legislature, one has to be selective in presenting the multiple views or approaches to the study of legislative policy-making.

Many scholars, including Malcolm Jewell and Samuel Patterson (1966:10), who study the legislative system, observe its flexibility, its ability to accommodate differences in ideology and interests and provide legislation that temporarily meets the needs of the political climate in a multiethnic environment. Charles Jones (1984:2), on the other hand, focuses on the policy process and how circumstances and changes in the political system affect the policy process. The point, according to Jones, is rather to illustrate the importance of how decisions are made. Whose advice was sought? How was the advice delivered? What questions were asked? How was the giving of advice managed? Who had the final say? He sees the system, its components, and the interaction between them as the key factor in the dynamics of the public policy process. In essence, these scholars emphasize different foci, but they all note the malleable and resilient nature of the role of Congress in the policy-making process.

Kenneth Boulding, in describing policy-making, states the following:

> In a sense, in a successful political process, all decisions are interim. We live in a perpetual state of unresolved conflict. A decision is a partial resolution of conflict. It is never a complete resolution. Of direct importance is that the majority does not rule, a majority decision is simply a setting of terms under which the minority continues discussion; a discussion which presumably goes on for at least the life time of the organization (1956:103).

The Act under study (Title VII) affects minorities directly; therefore, the representation and integration functions of Congress become essential. Accessibility, flexibility, and adaptability also become crucial if a successful integration is to be attained. The complex nature and the difficult role of Congress in policy-making is captured by Hans Morgenthau when he notes,

> The national interest is a compromise of conflicting political interests. It is not an ideal that is arrived at abstractly and scientifically, but a product of constant internal political competition (1958:65).

By focusing on the relationship between legislative functions, processes, and the internal and external political environments which constrain legislative actions, many scholars are able to provide an insight into the chores of a legislator. William Okeefe and Morris Ogul (1977) contend that in order for one to understand the legislature, a look at what it does and how it does it is mandatory. Notably, the key function of the legislature is law-making. But it also engages in other central functions such as checking the administration, providing political education for the public, providing representation, judicial function (impeachment), and leadership selection.

Similarly, Walter Oleszek, in discussing the legislative process, emphasizes the environmental constraints on Congress and asserts that

> In making their legislative decisions, members of Congress are influenced by numerous pressures—from their constituents, the White House, the media, lobbyists, organized interest groups, their own party leadership, and their colleagues on Capitol Hill. These pressures are a central feature of the congressional environment; they affect the formal procedures and rules of Congress. All these pressures are present in varying degrees in every step of the legislative process, the interests and influence of groups of individuals outside Congress have a considerable impact on the fate of a bill on Capitol Hill (1978:35).

The basic thrust of inquiry into the role of the legislature lies in the examination of its functions, processes, and political environment. These foci of descriptive policy analysis constitute what is commonly referred to as a "functional process" approach. However, this approach does not holistically deal with the study of the legislature. Other scholars also study Congress by looking at the congressional-bureaucratic interaction, otherwise known as the "institutional" approach.

One of these studies by Randall Ripley and Grace Franklin (1987) emphasizes the importance of interaction between bureaucrats and members of Congress. This interaction is constitutionally mandated because of separate institutions with shared powers. The three branches of government are both separate and intertwined by the interaction and cooperation necessary for a successful policy formulation. The nature of this interaction is characterized by either conflict or cooperation. But as Ripley and Franklin put it in this brief summary,

> The premium is placed on the production of policy that is usually an extension of the status quo or some incremental variant of it. More policy production also creates more bureaucracy, which in the course of implementing programs creates more occasions for members of Congress to serve their constituents in dealing with the bureaucracy (1987:13).

It is important to note that while most studies of the legislature and its interaction with other governmental institutions focus on the conflicts that ensue, most of the laws passed by Congress are a result of compromise between these separate institutions with shared powers. The incremental nature of American public policy processes, the continuous and endless nature of these policy processes, the number of actors—both inside and outside the government, the multiple decision points, and the growth of government services and functions, not to mention the personal interests of the legislators, have made the role of Congress more complex to understand.

These complex, unstable, and everburgeoning processes are what Woodrow Wilson aptly referred to as "The dance of legislation" (1956:195).

Another group of scholars has studied Congress by looking at the personal interests or motives of the legislators, and asking who really makes American policies. These scholars include Thomas Dye and Harman Zeigler (1975), David Mayhew (1975), Morris Fiorina (1977), Charles Clapp (1964), Peter Bachrach (1966), and Michael Parenti (1983).

The scholars in this group utilize elite theory in their analyses of Congress. A common theme in their studies is that the elite (including legislators) and their personal interests determine the role of the legislature in policy-making. As Dye and Zeigler bluntly put it, "Elites, not masses, govern America." They went further to define elite as the few who have power, and the masses as the many who do not (1975:1-3).

One of the characteristics of the elite is its desire to acquire and maintain power. Similarly, congressmen, once elected, tend to want to stay in office by seeking re-election. The principal motivation of congressmen, according to Mayhew, is re-election. This electoral connection affects not only their own behavior and accountability, but also the structure of Congress and the way it makes public policies. The core of Mayhew's study hinges upon the assumption that "United States congressmen are interested in getting re-elected—indeed, in their role here as abstractions, interested in nothing else" (1975:13). Fiorina, on the other hand, presents an indictment on the role of Congress in perpetuating a triangle of self-interest and ignoring important national issues to ensure continued re-election of its members. "The bureaucrats," he noted, "are not the problem, congressmen are.... The Congress created the establishment, sustain it, and most likely will continue to sustain and even expand it" (1977:3).

Parenti adds a political-economic twist to the elitist and "undemocratic" aspects of American public policy. However, he reaches the same conclusion when he asserts that

> Our government represents the privileged few rather than the many, and that participating in elections and activities of political parties and exercising the right to speak out are seldom effective measures against the influences of corporate wealth. The laws of our polity operate chiefly with undemocratic effect because they are written principally to advance the interests of the haves at the expense of the have-nots and because even if equitable as written, they usually are enforced in highly discriminatory ways (1983:2-3).

Parenti presents a plausible picture of the nature of democracy and policy-making in America. However, the elite theory is nothing new because the founding fathers of this nation have often been referred to as the nation's first elite. But the notable aspect of Parenti's work—the struggle for democracy by the masses—will constitute in part the basis for a thorough analysis of the politics of the 1968 Bilingual Education Act. The notion of the origin of the ruling elite or the status-quo of American public policy is captured by C. Wright Mills when he notes the following:

> From the beginning of the American Republic to modern times the great majority of those who occupied political offices of the nation—including the presidency and the vice presidency, the cabinet and the supreme court—have come from wealthy families (the upper 5 or 6 percent of the population), and most of the remainder have come from well-off middle class origins (moderately successful businessmen, commercial farmers, and professionals) (1956:400–402).

In support of the preceding argument, Bachrach insists that the present position of elites can be offset by revitalizing political participation. In order to accomplish this goal, he proposes a new definition of the "political," one that is sufficiently comprehensive to include the concentrations of private power, such as the giant corporations, whose decisions affect society as profoundly as the decisions of government itself. The next step is then to extend the idea and practice of democratic participation to these units (1966:ix–x). Bachrach's alternative approach leaves one with a difficult choice: either a revitalization of democratic participation or the acceptance of a state of affairs in which political decision-making is carried on with progressively less democratic control. After all, "Democracy can best be assured of survival by enlisting the people's support in a continual effort to make democracy meaningful in the lives of all men" (Bachrach 1966:106).

Clapp looks at the role of the legislature from the other side of the spectrum—the congressman's view. His analysis confirms other studies on the relative importance of personal motives in congressional behavior. Many congressmen spend their time getting re-elected. The net result of this quest for re-election is that the primary duty of the legislator (law-making) sometimes suffers or becomes secondary in the scheme of things. Congressional comments to Clapp tend to substantiate the validity of this indictment:

> You have a responsibility not only to yourself, but to your constituents, to get elected. The functions of your office that can legitimately be used to help you get

re-elected should be used. At least one third of our activities today are spent in working towards re-election. You know the saying, "you can't be a statesman unless you get elected" (1964:86).

The complex and difficult nature of the policy-making environment sometimes precludes logic and reason from determining policies. The unfortunate issue here is that lawmakers often fail to be knowledgeable on issues or matters of policy decision. However, they rely on clues from those who ought to know and incrementally cast a vote that is perhaps in their judgment politically popular. As Clapp notes, one former congressman sums up the problem this way:

> You've got to realize that not only are we sitting here trying to analyze legislation, trying to do the best job we can, but factors other than absolute reason are always entering the situation.... We are operating in a political environment, surrounded by lobbyists, constituents, the leadership, and jangling telephones and we virtually have no time alone to think and reflect upon the problems before us. The big miracle is that somehow, all of this works (1964:161).

Indeed, the foregoing discussion clearly indicates why it is important to examine the role of the legislature in the passage of the 1968 Bilingual Education Act. This will allow readers to get an idea of who has gained and who stands to gain from the power struggle that helped to shape the bilingual education policy.

Works on Political Systems Theory

The notion of political systems analysis can be traced back to David Easton's (1953) treatise of "the political system." Easton offered a major critique of the condition of political science as a discipline. He then went on to suggest the use of the "systems" concept as a valuable analytical tool for identifying integrally related aspects of concrete social reality that can be referred to as political.

In a subsequent work, Easton (1965b) borrowed heavily from the communications science of cybernetics to provide an analytical model for the study of all phenomena, physical and social, as behaving systems. His main purpose was to construct an empirically oriented general theory of politics by defining the kinds of functions characteristic of any political system. In order to do this, he examined the basic processes through which any type of political system persists as a system of behavior in a world either of stability or change. This analysis was based on four major aspects: (1) system, (2) environment, (3) response, and (4) feedback.

Easton further sought to endow the notion of the political system with teleological character in another work. He suggested that in its goal-setting, self-transforming, and creativity-adaptive strategy, the political system takes on a certain concreteness. He noted the "life processes of political systems" and argued that political analysis should be primarily devoted to understanding how political systems manage to persist through time (1965b:xi).

Lewis Coser (1956) argued that certain forms of conflict, rather than being dysfunctional, may actually be productive in that they may make important contributions to the maintenance of the entire system. Furthermore, Coser stated that conflict is useful when it establishes and reinforces the identity of groups within a system; and that reciprocal antagonism serves to maintain the total system by establishing a balance between various groups and component parts of the system.

Gabriel Almond (1960) employed the political system concept in his functional approach, as opposed to the more traditional "state" approach, which he found quite limited because of its legal and institutional connotations. Samuel Finer (1969–1970) found Almond's approach quite useful because it distinguished the political system in terms of a particular set of interactional properties, which, in turn, comprise comprehensiveness, existence of boundaries, and interdependence.

Richard Fenno (1962) employed systems analysis to investigate the Appropriations Committee of the United States House of Representatives. First, he suggested that "system" concerns the purposes or goals of the political system. He defined the purpose of the Committee as the allocation of money. His second suggestion was that "system" concerns identifying the units of the system. In other words, the Committee should have an established membership. His third suggestion was that "system" concerns the relationships between the system and the environment. For Fenno, the Committee was effective in dealing with the entire House of Representatives, which is a significant part of the Committee's environment. Finally, he suggested that "system" concerns how the units of the system interact. Here, Fenno suggested that high membership stability, consensus on goals, and an egalitarian attitude lead to a great deal of integration among members of the Committee.

James Klonoski (1967), in his review of Easton's systems analysis of political life, suggested that no matter what one's perception of Easton's framework may be, its outlook has been entrenched in modern political analysis. This is because, according to Klonoski, Easton's model makes political relationships explicit and self-conscious in that it helps in ordering the diffuse data of political life.

Bertram Gross (1967), in his review of Easton's approach, countered Klonoski's suggestion by arguing that the structural elements of the "system" are never explicitly articulated, and that the "black box" representing the authority structures of government remains shrouded in mystery. Gross' argument was based on the fact that while suggesting certain structural components of the political system, Easton never provided concepts required to analyze the concrete subsystems of the system.

Morton Kaplan (1967) argued that the sort of limitation pointed out by critics of the systems framework is not valid. According to Kaplan, if a theory for a system or type of system can be constructed as a system of equilibrium, then one can investigate how individual variations in the parameters produce deviant or unstable behavior within the system.

Herbert Spiro (1967) argued that the close relationship between systems analysis and structural-functional analysis opens up systems analysis to the very problems endemic in structural-functional analysis. Spiro suggested that the limitation of the system approach is its excessive preoccupation with stability: the maintenance of the status quo.

Oran Young (1968) called for the incorporation of functional analysis in the study of comparative political systems. His rationale was that functional analysis provides a set of standardized categories that can be applied successfully over widely disparate political systems.

Howard Scarrow (1969) emphasized Young's point when he suggested that the systems approach is closely related to functionalism in the sense that both are based on a conception of political phenomena as a system of interrelated and reciprocally regulated patterns of action and orientation. These patterns, suggested Scarrow, cluster together in equilibrium and have certain needs for survival and maintenance.

Leroy Rieselbach (1970) examined the United States Congress using the systems analysis approach. In his study, he found that the common thread that runs through all of the definitions of a political system is the emphasis on interaction. In addition, he found that a basic definition of system, given the United States Congress, is the interaction among definable units to achieve some purpose.

Eugene Miller (1971) suggested that the remarkable capacity to persist which Easton pointed out about political systems hinges largely on the way

Easton defined *persistence*: a concept heavily charged with the idea of stability. Thus, Miller argued that such a system is homeostatic to the point of self-transformation.

Reid Reading (1972), in his review of Easton's systems model, questioned how a system could endure for very long by relying solely on building up a reservoir of support. Reading argued, therefore, that while diffuse support may provide elasticity, the conditions under which such support come to rescue the system may be quite difficult, if not impossible, to generate.

In sum, the works examined here are clearly not definitive in their discourse on political behavior. Although the authors make strong arguments in support of or against the systems approach, the cumulative research is inconsistent and limited. The debate engendered in these works, nonetheless, act as stimuli to more research that will still undoubtedly add to the cumulative knowledge already established on political systems.

Research Method

This section presents a discussion of the methodological tools that were found useful for this book. Each of these tools is discussed in relationship to the 1968 Bilingual Education Act.

The Case Study Approach

In order to examine the research questions and dissect the politics of the 1968 Bilingual Education Act, a case study approach is utilized. This method represents a comprehensive description and explanation of the many components of the politics of bilingual education in the United States. Consequently, this method allowed for the collection and examination of as many data as possible on the issue.

This approach differs radically from causally oriented methods that aim at generalized understanding. It is directed at the understanding of a single idiosyncratic case: the politics of bilingual education in the United States. Whereas most approaches tend to limit the number of variables considered, the case study method seeks to maximize them. This qualitative approach was very useful in the sequential analysis of the subject matter. With this approach, it was possible to mix the specific and the general, the peculiar and the typical, the thematic and the descriptive by focusing on one set of legislative issues. The utility of this qualitative approach was augmented by the adoption of the slightly modified version of the Eastonian system framework for the political analysis that follows.

Theoretical Framework

The theoretical framework used and tested in this book is a slightly modified version of Easton's "framework for political analysis" in the sense that the major focus is on the American legislative system. This framework is diagrammatically represented as follows:

```
ENVIRONMENT                                        ENVIRONMENT

I                                                            O
N Demands→          THE              Decisions→              U
P                   LEGISLATIVE                              T
U Support→          SYSTEM           Action→                 P
T                                                            U
S                                                            T
↑                                                            S
├──────────────────── FEEDBACK────────────────────────┤

ENVIRONMENT                                        ENVIRONMENT
```

Figure 1. A slightly modified Model of the Political System provided by David Easton in *A Framework for Political Analysis* (Englewood Cliffs, New Jersey: Prentice-Hall, 1965a:112).

Easton's theoretical framework rests on four premises. The first is the **System**; that is, "it is useful to view political life as a system of behavior" (1965:25). For this book, this calls for the examination of the American political system in terms of the bargaining process which took place in Congress and between the Congress, the Executive, and the Judiciary in enacting the 1968 Bilingual Education Act.

The second premise of Easton's framework is the **Environment**. As he put it, "A system is distinguished from the environment in which it exists and open to influences from it" (1965a:25). In terms of this book, it means that the political, economic, social, and cultural environment within which the politics of the 1968 Bilingual Education Act was framed is analyzed.

The third premise in Easton's framework is **Response**: "Variations in the structures and processes within a system may usefully be interpreted as constructive or positive alternative efforts by members of a system to regulate or cope with stress flowing from environmental as well as internal sources" (1965b:26). For this book, this means that an examination of the manner in which Congress coped with conditions of the environment, in light of the sources that were available to it when it embarked upon formulating the 1968 Bilingual Education Act, is conducted.

The fourth premise is **Feedback**. According to Easton, feedback is "the capacity of a system to persist in the face of stress in a function of the presence and nature of the information and other influences that return to its actors and decision-makers" (1965b:26). This calls for analyzing various responses and/or actions of various groups that were affected by the passage of the Act under study.

Following Easton's conception, the systems analysis approach is beneficial for examining the role of the legislature in the passage of the 1968 Bilingual Education Act because the framework

> takes its departure from the notion of political life as a boundary-maintaining set of interactions imbedded in and surrounded by other social systems to the influence of which it is constantly exposed. As such, it is helpful to interpret political phenomena as constituting an open system, one that must cope with the problems generated by its exposure to influences from these environmental systems. If a system of this kind is to persist through time, it must obtain adequate feedback about its past performances, and it must be able to take measures that regulate its future behavior (Easton 1965b:25).

The pattern of analysis, then, involves the examination of the following variables:

1. the nature of the inputs,

2. the variable conditions under which they will constitute a stressful disturbance on the system,

3. the environmental and systemic conditions that generate such stressful conditions,

4. the typical ways in which systems have sought to cope with stress,

5. the role of information feedback, and finally,

6. the part that outputs play in these conversion and coping processes (Easton 1965b:132).

In sum, the systems analysis framework allows a researcher to conceive public policy as a response of a political system to forces brought to bear upon it from the environment. Forces generated in the environment which affect the political system are viewed as the **inputs**. The **environment** is any condition or circumstance defined as external to the boundaries of the political system. The political **system** (for this book, the legislative system) represents that group of interrelated structures and processes which functions authoritatively to allocate values for a society. **Outputs** of the political system are authoritative value allocations of the system, and these allocations constitute **public policy**.

The Data

Two types of data were collected for this book: primary and secondary data. These data were collected as follows:

Primary Data. Face-to-face interviews were conducted in order to solicit various perspectives on the passage of the 1968 Bilingual Education Act and its aftermath. The instrument employed to collect the data during the interviews generally entailed the following questions:

1. How would you describe the political, economic, social, and cultural climate of the country during the debate of the 1968 Bilingual Education Act?

2. What type of support did your organization extend to decision-makers during the debate?

3. What type of pressure and/or demand did your organization bring to bear on decisionmakers during the debate?

4. How would you characterize the positions and roles of the various branches of government during the debate?

5. How would you characterize the positions of other competing groups during the debate?

6. What do you believe were the major goals of the Act?

7. Were these goals congruent to those of your organization?

8. Do you believe that these goals have been met? If yes, how? If not, why?

9. What do you believe are the linkages between the Act and overall educational policy in the United States?

10. How would you describe your personal experience in the process of influencing the passage (or defeat) of the Act?

This combination of closed- and open-ended questions was posed so that respondents would describe their knowledge, experiences, feelings, beliefs, ideas, predispositions, and values about various aspects of the 1968 Bilingual Education Act. Thus, this instrument encompasses fact questions, opinion and attitude questions, information questions, and behavior questions.

These personal interviews were conducted in the respondents' offices and recorded on tape. Notes were also taken as deemed necessary.

In addition to a number of government officials working on bilingual/bicultural education programs, the directors of the following organizations were interviewed for the attendant reasons cited:

1. The National Clearinghouse for Bilingual Education (NACBE). Based in Arlington, Virginia, this organization is operated by the InterAmerica Research Associates, Inc. and funded by the Office of Bilingual Education and Minority Languages Affairs, United States Department of Education, to undertake projects that encourage researchers to express their judgment freely in professional and technical matters in a series of legislatively mandated studies on bilingual education.

2. Bilingual/Foreign Language Education (BFLE). Based in Dade County, Florida, BFLE was the first organization to initiate a bilingual education program in 1963. The program attracted national attention.

3. National Association for Bilingual Education (NABE). With headquarters in Washington, DC, this organization has emerged as the leading proponent of bilingual education in the United States. A number of NABE's writings and testimonies can be found in United States Congressional Records.

4. United States English (USE). Like NABE, USE's headquarters is based in Washington, DC, and has a number of writings and testimonies in United States Congressional Records. But unlike NABE, USE has emerged as the leading opponent of bilingual education in the United States. (Due to preliminary agreements reached with some of the interviewees, anonymity is preserved in presenting statements made by them.)

In addition to these interviews, the relevant Congressional Records on the bilingual issue were used as primary data sources. These records entail congressional debates and testimonies which allow a researcher to delineate the legislative history as well as the politics of the 1968 Bilingual Education Act. Specifically, these records were elicited from the 89th and 90th Congresses and covered the period from 1965 to 1968.

Secondary Data. Books, journal articles, newspaper articles, and magazine articles that deal with the issue of the 1968 Bilingual Education Act were consulted. These sources also covered the areas of public policy-making, legislative processes, systems analysis theory, and thus allow a researcher to discern other perspectives on the Act.

As mentioned earlier, the data collected from these sources were analyzed qualitatively. This means that a comprehensive description and explanation of the data collected was called for.

Organization of the Rest of the Book

The following chapter (two) focuses on the political, social, economic, and cultural environment in which the legislation under study was passed. The discussion of these environmental conditions form the basis for the analysis of the political system. The consequent exercise examines how these environmental forces impacted on the political process in general, and the legislature in particular.

In chapter three, the inputs, that is, demands, pressures, and support of the various groups within the political system, are examined. This chapter details how these inputs set off the political process that led to the 1968 Bilingual Education Act. Attention is paid to the key actors that participated in articulating the demands, support, and pressure that came to bear on the legislators.

Chapter four looks at the legislative system within which the Act was passed. It highlights the transformational process or the politics of the legislation. The integral part of the process—bargaining, conflict, cooperation, and lawmaking—is examined in this chapter. The hearings, the haggling, and the debate that ensued in Congress constitute part of this analysis. A clear picture of how a bill becomes a law or the "dance of legislation" is presented here, along with the functions of the legislature.

The outputs of the 1968 Bilingual Education Act and its subsequent amendments are the objects of discussion in chapter five. The Act is discussed in detail and both the spirit and the letter of the law are examined. An attempt is made to evaluate the relation between the inputs and the outputs to determine how the Act represents the demands of the political environment.

In chapter six, the entire study is tied together by summary and conclusions. An examination of the legislative process and a presentation of the findings of the study form the core of this chapter. An appraisal of the 1968 Bilingual Education Act, the politics of legislation, and Easton's framework for political analysis is conducted as part of this final chapter. Also, some recommendations are suggested for future policies.

Chapter 2

ENVIRONMENT

This chapter presents a discussion of the environment within which the 1968 Bilingual Education Act was passed. More specifically, the discussion centers on the political, economic, social, and cultural environment within which the legislation was enacted. An examination of the environment is necessary because, as Easton states, it lies "outside the society of which the political system itself is a social sub-system; yet it may have important consequences for the persistence or change of a political system" (1965a:73).

In essence, Easton argues that political life is open to influences from its environment. He therefore insists that the political system is an open system, not a closed system as some others may be inclined to suggest. The whole idea is to focus on the entire system of political life by separating it from the environment. By so doing, the impact of the environment on the political system becomes crystal clear. According to Ronald Chilcote, "these influences emanate from the physical environment (topography, geographical dispersion of nations); the nonhuman organic environment (flora, fauna); and the social environment (people, their actions and reactions)" (1981:146).

The constant interaction between the system and the environment is responsible for its persistence. Congress, of course, is not insulated from the environment. Therefore, when stress occurs within the environment, it impacts on the system. In the case of the Bilingual Education Act, it is not possible to account for the total environmental factors, but only those with "potential effectiveness." Easton divides the environment of a political system into two categories: the intrasocietal and the extrasocietal. These environments are open to multiple transactions that take place within the system, and between the system and the total environment. These transactions or influences or stress on the environment affect inputs and outputs. Influences within the system that result in outputs are referred to as "withputs" (1965:23–25). Due to the multiple influence from the environment, Congress oftentimes broker the various stress factors. The government therefore, in most cases, has shown a limited response to stimuli of signals of unrest, thus allowing the demands to continue and sustain the system.

By conducting a diligent, protracted, and in-depth investigation into the system's environment, the impact of those factors on the Bilingual Education Act becomes ubiquitous in all phases of this book. The social, economic, political, and cultural environment of the Bilingual Education Act was shaped by the basic foundation of American democracy which dates back to the Declaration of Independence in 1776.

> ...That all men are endowed by their Creator with certain unalienable rights.... Life, liberty, and the pursuit of happiness...that governments are instituted among men, deriving their just powers from the consent of the governed that whenever any form of government becomes destructive of these ends, it is the right of the people to alter or to abolish it, institute new government,...and to provide new guards for their future security (Todd and Curti 1977:108).

Each person within the systems environment is endowed to live his/her life according to his/her beliefs and has an equal voice in the decisions that affect him/her and the entire system. The notion of equality is a slippery concept because it is very difficult if not impossible to legislate equality. The political implication of such a system founded on equality of all men is that the variables used to gauge equality—income, social status, influence, wealth, etc.—cannot actually be equalized in any given society. The system, in the face of this dilemma, attempts to provide its citizens with the next best thing to ideal equality—equal opportunity. As Roland Pennock notes,

> the objective of this equality (of power) is not merely the recognition of a certain dignity of the human being as such, but it is also to provide him with the opportunity—equal to that guaranteed to others—for protecting and advancing his interests and developing his powers and personality (1962:12607).

However, equality of opportunity does not necessarily guarantee ideal equality. This is due in part to the manipulative abilities of the elite and the fragile composition of the political environment. According to Harold Lasswell, "the fate of the elite is profoundly affected by the ways it manipulates the environment, that is to say, by use of violence, goods, symbols, and practices" (1936:103). By virtue of this elite manipulative power, equality slips away and only a few get most of the values within the system. This endemic problem of a pluralistic society was high-lighted by Michael Parenti in "Democracy for the Few" (1983) and E. E. Schattschneider when he noted that "the flaw in the pluralist haven is that the heavenly chorus sings with a strong upper class accent" (1960:35).

The social, political, economic, and cultural environment of the 1960s, leading to the passage of the Bilingual Education Act of 1968 centers around the struggle for or the demand for equal opportunity and on the notion that "all men are created equal." It is important to note the interrelation or lack of dichotomy between these environmental variables. They all deal with the authoritative allocation of scarce resources or values; and in Lasswell's terms, "who gets what, when and how" (1936:103). The sociocultural standing within the systems environment to some extent depends on the political-economic power position of the relevant groups or individuals in the polity.

By conducting a diligent, protracted, and an in-depth investigation into the systems environment, it becomes obvious that the mood of the nation in the 1960s played a major role in the passage of the Bilingual Education Act. Due to vast activities in the environment during this period, this book focuses on those environmental factors that have potential effectiveness. Based on personal interviews, there was a consensus that during this period, the Civil Rights Movement and the great awakening of the American people to the ills of the society was a key political issue. The concept of equality under the law became prevalent in all facets of the American polity. Emphasis on equality of economic, political, social, and cultural opportunity dominated the society's discourse particularly among the disadvantaged. There was an enormous stress in the political environment among the invisible minority or those that felt disenfranchised.

The utopian society that presumably followed the depression of earlier years vanished quickly as poverty re-emerged in various facets of the American society. A bifocal view of the American nation was existing in the 1960s. From a distance, everything that depicted prosperity—high-rise buildings, monuments, highways, etc.—were visible. But, close up, there existed poverty, crime, homelessness, hopelessness, etc., and many people lived lives of quiet desperation. The nation was economically sound at this time but this affluence excluded many people, thereby creating an enormous stress in the environment.

The rosy economy and the affluence of the 1960s were echoed in policy statements and pronouncements by both the Kennedy and the Johnson Administrations. Phrases like the "New Frontier" and "The Great Society" were often used to portray the euphoria that existed in the nation during this period. A vivid picture of the general feeling of confidence in "the Great Society" was the theme of President Johnson's State of the Union message in 1965:

> ...Most important of all...the United States has re-emerged into the fullness of its self-confidence and purpose. No longer are we called upon to get America moving. We are moving. No longer do we doubt our strength or resolution. We are strong and we have proven our resolve. No longer can anyone wonder whether we are in the grip of historical decay. We know that history is ours to make. And if there is great danger, there is now also the excitement of great expectations (excerpt from President Lyndon B. Johnson's Address to a Joint Session of the House and Senate, January 4, 1965).

Despite the general feeling of affluence notably in mainstream America, the fact remained that many Americans outside the mainstream were excluded from the dividends of this affluence. This prompted the Johnson Administration to embark upon what some referred to as a "legislative revolution." Many landmark laws in the area of civil rights, education, medical care, immigration, housing, and antipoverty (collectively known as the Great Society Programs) were passed during the Johnson years. These programs were jeopardized by the Vietnam War and the hopes of the minorities turned into frustration and caused even more stress on the social-political environment.

A discussion of the sociopolitical mood and the environment of the 1960s prior to the passage of the Bilingual Education Act cannot be complete without recognizing the impact of the war in Southeast Asia on the United States. As a result of the cost of the war, the Great Society Programs, mostly aimed at the nation's poor and at correcting the social ills of the system, were vitiated. The affluent great society unfortunately found itself in a dilemma as the war raged in Vietnam and disorder, discontent, frustration, and social avalanche dominated the home front. The cost of financing this war changed the social, political, and economic climate of the nation and inhibited the implementation of the legislative revolution of the Johnson Administration. The "War on Poverty" took a back seat to the Vietnam War and some people lost faith in the promise of applying political solutions to social problems.

The sociopolitical environment was cluttered by stiff opposition to the war in Southeast Asia. There were riots in the ghettos and college campuses across the nation in opposition to both the war and the socioeconomic condition of the nation. As part of the President's response to these stresses in the environment, he opted not to seek re-election. The Vietnam War was and is still the most unpopular war in the history of this nation because of its timing, consequence, and result. However, the hallmark of the Great Society's legislative revolution was its recognition of the other America—that is, the plight of millions of poor Americans barred from the dividends of the affluent society. History also recorded this realization of poverty amidst affluence, putting it on the national agenda, and passing legislation to rectify these inequities as part of President Johnson's major domestic policy achievements. Notably, the Bilingual Education Act was a by-product of the New Deal and the Great Society Programs of the 1960s.

A case was made for the social, economic, and political environment of the 1960s and the inequities that existed by John Kenneth Galbraith in his book, *The Affluent Society* (1976). In this book, Galbraith contends that poverty was still a big problem amidst affluence and was concentrated in certain segments of the country. More disturbing in his analysis is the fact that some people are required to stay permanently poor so that others may stay permanently rich. The affluent society, he contends, "excludes numerous people from its endowment" (1976:xii–xiii). Galbraith estimates that about 24 percent of the population lived in either "case poverty" or "insular poverty." Those classified under case poverty are poor due to some individual handicap or characteristics peculiar to the individual while the insular poor are those left out and technically live in an "island" of poverty. People in this group were frustrated by some factors in their environment and are thus permanently poor (Galbraith 1976:234–235).

Equally provocative is another book by Michael Harrington, entitled *The Other America: Poverty in the United States* (1963). In this book, Harrington vividly describes the plight of about 50,000,000 poor Americans whom he referred to as the rejects of the affluent society who live in the other American segment of the richest country on earth. Inclusive in this population are "the unskilled workers, the migrant farm workers, the aged, and the minorities who live in the economic underworld of American life" (1963:10). America became blind to the plight of the poor and thus created institutionalized poverty, thereby, causing enormous stress on the environment.

These two books along with many other publications highlighted the socioeconomic and political mood of the country that many believed brought poverty and inequality on the national agenda and set off the war on poverty.

There was also at this time a sense of ethnic identity and a rise of social and cultural awareness among the various groups of the great society.

Also on the rise was the political consciousness among African Americans, Hispanics, and other minority groups. The commonly used category of white, black, or other did not suffice any longer because of the demands of various minority groups for equal representation. There was a need for an agenda that includes this invisible minority and takes into account the new trends in immigration. For example, during an interview conducted on June 15, 1992 with Dr. A. Gomez, the Director of the National Clearinghouse for Bilingual Education (NACBE), he revealed that the Spanish-speaking population at this time was about twenty million. The socio-political impact of this new demographic development obviously factored in the environment leading to the passage of the Bilingual Education Act in 1968. It is not surprising therefore that the push for Bilingual Education legislation primarily emanated from states like Texas, Florida, and California with large Hispanic populations. It is important to note here that the Bilingual Education Act was aimed at providing equal opportunity in education of minorities and, thus, provide economic, social, political, cultural, and other opportunities equal to those provided to others within the affluent society.

In order to seek redress for these inequities, African Americans, Hispanics, and other minorities held demonstrations and marches to protest unemployment, poor housing, inadequate representation in government, insular and case poverty, lack of economic opportunity, and inability to share in the American dream. These protest activities opened up debates across the nation. The issue at hand was political justice and the notion that "all men are created equal." The sociopolitical climate in the environment dictated that measures be taken to correct or rectify these inequities in order to reduce stress. In response to this environmental stress, the government introduced remedies which included but were not limited to medicare, war on poverty, the Voting Rights Act, the Civil Rights Act of 1964, the Economic Opportunity Act (ESEA) of the same year, and the Elementary and Secondary Education Act of 1965. In 1968, the ESEA was amended. It later became Title VII or the Bilingual Education Act which is the focus of this book. Section 702 of this Act (P.L. 90-247) states that

> In recognition of the special educational needs of the large number of children of
> limited English-speaking ability in the United States, Congress hereby declares it to
> become the policy of the United States to provide financial assistance to local

educational agencies to develop and carry out new and imaginative elementary and secondary school programs designed to meet these special educational needs. For the purpose of this Title, children of limited English ability means children who come from environments where the dominant language is other than English.

If there is one aspect on which supporters and opponents of bilingual education are in agreement, it is the notion that the period from the early to mid-1960s was one of the most exciting times in modern America history. Civil rights activists were staging interracial sit-ins, marches, and freedom rides. The Rev. Dr. Martin Luther King, Jr. was championing the crusade for equal rights. The folk singer, Bob Dylan, was composing memorable songs for peace and justice. Chief Justice Earl Warren was leading the Supreme Court toward breakthrough decisions, broadening the Bill of Rights. John F. Kennedy, appearing youthful, articulate, and energetic, was occupying the White House. Despite his assassination in November 1963, many progressives kept hope alive. Under the Johnson Administration, many remarkably wide-ranging reforms were enacted. The 1960s, it seemed, would see the triumph of social justice in the United States.

Political Environment: The Presidency

The Kennedy Era, 1960–1963

The 1960s began with Kennedy occupying the White House. Kennedy exalted activity and vigor almost as ends in themselves and insisted that the United States compete strenuously against its opponents. He saw himself as an "idealist without illusions" and clothed his doubts in an altruistic rhetoric that captured the mood of the time: "Ask not what your country can do for you. Ask what you can do for your country" (Patterson 1976:412).

Kennedy deliberately rejected Eisenhower's low-key approach in pursuing his (Kennedy) objectives. Kennedy revealed that he was prepared to use the tools in his command and that opponents could expect retaliation from the White House. He moved quickly to replace Eisenhower's businessmen with a group of academicians, intellectuals, and dynamic younger executives (who came to be referred to as "the best and brightest"), and rejected the staff system. His sense of humor brought favorable responses from the news media. Reporters welcomed his articulateness and his accessibility. Kennedy enjoyed great advantages in the television age of the 1960s due to his poise and good looks (Patterson 1976:412–413).

These assets helped the President in his early dealings with a very conservative Congress. In early 1961, he was able to get the Congress to liberalize the obstructive Rules Committee by a narrow margin of 217 to 212. In addition, Kennedy got Congress to increase the federal minimum wage, set aside funds for manpower training and area redevelopment, and pass a trade expansion act that sought to reduce tariffs throughout the Western industrialized world. Before his assassination in 1963, he got Congress to approve a multibillion-dollar tax cut, which was later passed by the Senate early in 1964. This was a Keynesian approach that risked short-term budgetary deficits in the hope of promoting purchasing power. By embracing this unorthodox idea, Kennedy showed his flexibility in dealing with major national issues (Patterson 1976:413–414). This early activism, however, was soon replaced with a relatively more cautious approach, due to the political realities facing the President at the time.

The political climate was simply not conducive for some of the major programs Kennedy had favored. This was because of three major factors: (1) lack of reliable progressive majorities in the Congress, (2) lack of support from pressure groups, and (3) lack of a popular mandate as expressed at the polls. Consequently, congressmen paid more attention to well-organized constituents rather than to presidential persuasion (Patterson 1976:415).

Another major political obstacle for Kennedy was the Roman Catholic Church. As a Catholic, he had to deny aid to parochial and private schools. Otherwise, angry Protestants would have accused him of religious favoritism. The President's decision, as to be expected, led prominent Catholic churchmen to oppose his 1961 education bill (Patterson 1976:415).

The power of big business, which sought to maintain the status quo, made the political climate more turbulent for the President, even though he sought to conciliate these corporate leaders. To demonstrate his sincerity, Kennedy appointed Douglas Dillon, a prominent banker who had served as an Under-Secretary of State in the Eisenhower Administration, as Secretary of the Treasury, and Robert McNamara, head of the Ford Motor Company, as Secretary of Defense. But, these appointments did not win over uneasy business leaders. When stockmarket prices dipped, these business leaders were quick to blame the President (Patterson 1976:415).

The political climate was so tense that many progressives came to believe that the President had shied away from promoting controversial social programs. He had hoped that by avoiding confrontations, he would win a massive victory in 1964 that would give him the necessary mandate he needed for his second term. This approach led him to rely on congressional leaders like Speaker of the House Sam Rayburn or Senators Richard Russell of Georgia and Everett Dirksen of Illinois, the GOP leader, for his programs (Patterson 1976:416–417).

Kennedy was also quite cautious in dealing with civil rights matters, although he showed a great deal of sympathy for the movement. For African Americans, however, there was a revolution of rising expectations. Since 1940, millions had either joined the armed forces or moved to the North. There, they began to escape the poverty and isolation that had prevented collective actions in the past. But even in the North, African Americans encountered a subtler brand of racism that exposed with greater clarity the Jim Crow system of the South. Supreme Court decisions like *Brown v Board of Education* in 1954 had led African Americans to hope, albeit briefly, that the revolution was on the way. But Kennedy's cautious moves in the 1960s made it obvious to African Americans that legal protection was not enough; only direct action could promote social justice (Patterson 1976:418).

In February 1960, young people popularized direct-action tactics by staging sit-ins at segregated lunch counters in the South. In April of that year, the Student Nonviolent Coordinating Committee (SNCC) joined the rapidly growing Congress on Racial Equality (CORE), King's Southern Christian Leadership Conference (SCLC), and the National Association for the Advancement of Colored People (NAACP) in the struggle for equal rights. By May 1961, CORE members were staging integrated freedom rides into the South in efforts to desegregate transportation terminals. The participants in these acts were thoroughly beaten (and some died as a result) by angry white mobs in the process. In 1962, James Meredith, an African American, tried to enroll in the University of Mississippi, only to be confronted by Governor Ross Barnett and by angry white crowds. In a night of campus violence, two people were killed and 375 injured, including 166 federal marshals. When King led nonviolent demonstrations in Birmingham, Alabama in April 1963, Police under Eugene "Bull" Conner repelled demonstrators with electric cattle prods, water hoses, and dogs. The incidents, shown on nationwide television, resulted into a wave of sympathy for King's cause in the North (Patterson 1976:417).

A number of factors combined to encourage the activities of direct-action tactics. First, there was the dramatic television coverage that such methods attracted. Second, the young demonstrators held a basic idealism of fearlessness because they were impatient with what they considered the miscalculations of politicians and the legalism of groups such as the NAACP. Finally, King, a spellbinding speaker with a deep Christian faith, evoked ready responses among African Americans in the South. Many whites also saw King as "safe" because of his doctrine of nonviolence, suggesting that they need not fear race war (Patterson 1976:417). The young demonstrators also came to realize that the NAACP Legal Defense Fund was indispensable, as they were constantly being arrested (Leuchtenburg 1973:99).

By mid-1963, the actions of segregationists forced Kennedy to move more purposefully than he had before. Aroused to action, the President urged the passage of a civil rights law. Faced with congressional dawdling, he acquiesced in a plan by activists for a march on Washington in August. The march, which attracted over 200,000 supporters, went off peacefully. King, as featured speaker, told participants and the millions watching on television that he had a "dream, chiefly rooted in the American dream." "One day on the red hills of Georgia," he prophesied, "the sons of former slaves and the sons of former slave-owners will be able to sit at the table of brotherhood" (Patterson 1976:419).

But the political climate remained so volatile that even during the final days of his life, Kennedy failed to grasp the intensity behind the drive for racial justice. His proposed civil rights bill was very weak. It contained no provision on fair employment practices, and limited the Justice Department's injunctive powers against racial discrimination in education (Patterson 1976:420).

The Kennedy years, it seemed, were marked by the lack of a clear national purpose. As Director of the National Association for Bilingual Education (NABE), Jim Lyons suggested during an interview conducted on October 23, 1992 for this book, that too many people were trapped in poverty. Too many Americans were blighted by lack of opportunity, racial and religious prejudices abound; government and large business invaded citizens' personal freedom; cities were marred by juvenile delinquency and social disintegration; corruption and misuse of power were everywhere; and mediocrity in every phase of national life was the norm.

As MacGregor Burns observed, the American political environment was characterized by "deadlock," broken only by brief intervals of activity during the Kennedy years. As Burns further states,

We are at the critical stage of a somber and inexorable cycle that seems to have gripped the public affairs of the nation. We are mired in governmental deadlock, as Congress blocks or kills not only most of Mr. Kennedy's bold proposals of 1960,

but many planks of the Republican platform as well. Soon we will be ca'
politics of drift, as the nation's politicians put off major decisions until after un
presidential campaign of 1964 (1963:2).

Indeed, as one of the government officials interviewed for this book observed, the political climate during the Kennedy years was quite somber. This official went on to add that relations between the President and a Congress even controlled by his own party were so strained that prompt and decisive action was institutionally impossible. But, this mood was soon to give way to the most productive congressional session in American history.

The Johnson Era, 1963–1968

In November 1963, Kennedy's assassination in Dallas, Texas brought Vice President Lyndon B. Johnson to the White House. Johnson was one of the least likeable men to have occupied the White House. By the late 1960s, numerous stories had circulated about his towering ego, his crudity, and his cruelty to members of his staff. The President was reported to have once asked a friend why people did not like him. The friend replied: "Because, Mr. President, you are not a very likeable man." Once he publicly called his Press Secretary, George Reedy, a "stupid son-of-a-bitch." He raged at another aide, Jack Valenti, "I thought I told you, Jack, to fix this fucking doorknob...Where the goddam hell have you been?" (Patterson 1976:427).

In addition, liberals did not trust Johnson for a number of reasons. In 1948 when he squeaked into the Senate by eighty-seven votes, he worked with conservatives of the Eisenhower Administration who found him uncooperative. He was also seen as an assiduous protector of southwestern oil interests, a less than enthusiastic supporter of the civil rights movement, a wheeler and dealer, and a back-room storyteller like a river boat gambler with the drawl and the swagger of a Texas tycoon (Patterson 1976:427).

These early portrayals, however, ignored the political environment within which Johnson was operating at the time. He had to alienate liberals, not because he was instinctively conservative, but because he had to cater to the whims of his constituency in Texas. In fact, he had begun his political career as an ardent proponent of the New Deal in the 1930s. Even President Roosevelt regarded Johnson as potential presidential material. From 1954 to 1960, Johnson became a very effective Senate majority leader. Feeling more secure of his political base, Johnson began to accept many liberal programs. Without his patient negotiations on Capitol Hill, the civil rights bill of 1957, for example, could not have become law (Patterson 1976:427).

Johnson had advantages Kennedy lacked. To begin with, Johnson had friendships with many powerful congressmen like Richard Russell of Georgia and Harry Byrd of Virginia, who had little reason to help Kennedy. It was harder for many congressmen to be obstructive, given Johnson's many years' standing as a crony. His southern background made his support for civil rights quite impressive. As a Protestant, he was in a better position than Kennedy to tackle the issue of aid to parochial schools. More important, Johnson came to office at a time of national crisis: Kennedy's assassination. The nation was once again yearning for purposeful leadership (Patterson 1976:428).

Johnson was quick to take advantage of the country's mood at the time. Five days after Kennedy's assassination, Johnson assumed the former's new frontier programs. He appeared before Congress and reminded its members that civil rights was still an unfinished business.

With breathtaking results, Johnson was successful in getting Congress to pass many of Kennedy's programs. In 1964, Congress approved the $13.5 billion tax cut Kennedy had requested in June 1963. It enacted a controversial mass-transit bill, an $800 million "War Against Poverty" program, and the first effective civil rights bill since Reconstruction. The Civil Rights Act of 1964 made possible the inauguration of the Fair Employment Practices Committee, the banning of discrimination in public accommodations, and gave the Attorney General injunctive powers in school segregation and voting rights cases. It also authorized the government to withhold funds from public authorities practicing racial discrimination (Patterson 1976:429).

Given the political climate of the country at the time, these programs would have been passed in any event. However, Johnson made a great difference. For example, although the poverty program was conceived during the final weeks of Kennedy's presidency, Johnson had to give it its shape and scope.

As if to ensure Johnson's re-election to the White House, the Republicans nominated Senator Barry Goldwater of Arizona to challenge the President in the 1964 election. Goldwater, a reactionary who opposed civil rights legislation and progressive federal taxation, and had called for the bombing of Vietnam, was hailed by right-wingers. He even antagonized moderate Republicans at the GOP convention by courting support from the right-wing John Birch Society. Goldwater's nomination clearly signaled a major trend for the future: the rise of ideology (especially conservatism) in the American political arena. Johnson took advantage of Goldwater's positions on the issues, calling them irresponsible. To no one's surprise, Goldwater was thoroughly defeated in the election by 43.1 million to 27.1 million votes. Goldwater only won Arizona and five southern states. Once moribund in Dixie, the GOP now appeared wrecked everywhere else. The Democratic Party also enjoyed a tremendous coattail effect at the polls. It secured huge majorities of 68 to 32 in the Senate and 295 to 140 in the House. The enormous shifts in voting revealed that the political environment was becoming unpredictable and unstable in presidential elections (Patterson 1976:429–430).

Johnson, as is to be expected, interpreted his re-election as a clear mandate for further domestic reform. At a furious pace, Congress responded with the most far-reaching legislation since 1935. The major accomplishments included medicare and aid to elementary and secondary schools. With continued vigor, Congress also approved a number of reforms in 1965: appropriated generously for manpower training, authorized $900 million to improve conditions in Appalachia, passed the housing act, set aside $1.6 million more for the war against poverty, established the Economic Development Act for depressed areas with the potential for growth, created the Department of Housing and Urban Development and the National Endowment for the Arts and the Humanities, authorized an additional $2.4 billion for education, and approved a new immigration law ending quotas based on pseudo-scientific theories. As new outrage exploded because police in Selma, Alabama had roughed up African Americans seeking to register to vote, Johnson prodded Congress to approve the 1965 Civil Rights Act. This far-reaching law banned literacy tests and authorized federal examiners to register voters (Patterson 1976:430–431). It now appeared that Johnson, once disliked by the liberals, had become the greatest champion of the progressives.

This change of mood in the political environment affected Congress profoundly. Between 1966 and 1968, the lawmakers increased the minimum wage, created a Department of Transportation, established a Model Cities program, and approved another civil rights bill that sought to wipe out discrimination in housing (Patterson 1976:432).

In contrast to the Kennedy years, the Johnson years brought to fruition a generation's backlog of social legislation and ideas. Congress expressed the national purpose in bold and concrete terms, and the people overwhelmingly approved. In the words of the *Congressional Record*, "It is the Congress of accomplished hopes. It is the Congress of realized dreams" (US Congress 1965:28694–28695). Johnson's conduct in office was overwhelmingly approved by the people, as reported in public-opinion polls (American Institute of Public Opinion release, November 5, 1965). As one official of the District of Columbia Bilingual/Bicultural Education Program interviewed on June 25, 1992 for this book stated, "President Johnson's landslide election in 1964, which also brought into office an overwhelming and confident Democratic Congress, made the political environment plausible for quick policy action for a time."

Economic Environment

An examination of the *Economic Report of the President* for 1975 reveals that the United States economy grew steadily from 1961 to 1968. As Table 1 on the following page shows, the national product and income of the country increased steadily during this period. As a result, per capita disposable income also grew at a similar pace. An analysis of the economic situation is essential to the environment because the civil unrest preceding the Civil Rights Movement was caused mainly by economic depression and poverty. Also, there is a plausible relationship between education and economic opportunity, which is the underlying reason for the push for bilingual education programs (to provide equal opportunity for LEP and NEP students).

According to Emma Woytinsky (1967:133), personal consumption expenditures for goods and services constituted the main item of the country's national product and income. About 45 to 47 percent of personal expenditure went for purchase of nondurable goods, such as food, fuel, clothing, etc.; services absorbed somewhat less, and the remainder was used for the purchase of durable goods.

The remaining third of the GNP was accounted for by expenditures for (a) gross private domestic investment, such as new construction, purchase of producers' durable equipment, and inventories; (b) government purchases of goods and services, such as national defense, compensation of public employees, government enterprises, and net government purchases overseas. The federal government accounted for the largest part of government purchases, and national defense took nearly 75 percent of that sum. Net exports of goods and services represented a minor part (less than one percent) of the GNP (Woytinsky 1967:133).

Table 1

Economic Growth in the United States, 1961–1968

National Product and Income
(in billions of current dollars)

Year	GNP	PGN	NAI	DPI	PDC
1961	520.1	+3.2	427.3	364.4	1,984
1962	560.3	+7.7	457.7	385.3	2,065
1963	590.5	+5.4	481.9	404.6	2,138
1964	632.4	+7.1	518.1	438.1	2,283
1965	684.9	+8.3	564.3	473.2	2,436
1966	749.9	+9.5	620.6	511.9	2,604
1967	793.9	+5.9	653.6	546.3	2,749
1968	864.2	+8.9	711.1	591.0	2,945

GNP is Gross National Product, PGN is Percent Change from GNP of Preceding Year, NAI is National Income, DPI is Disposable Personal Income, and PDC is Per Capita Disposable Income (in current dollars). Source: Adapted from the *Economic Report of the President*, 1975:249, 267, 269.

Labor's share of the national income—that is, salaries and wages, including employers' contributions to social security, pensions of various kinds, renumerations and bonuses of executives, etc.—accounted for about 70 percent of the total in 1960–1965. The course of proprietors' income ran in the opposite direction from that of labor: it was about 11 percent in the 1960s. The principal decline was for farmers, whose share in national income fell from 6.5 percent in 1945 to three percent or less in the 1960s. The share of corporate profits fluctuated between 11 and 13 percent of the national income. The share of net interest and that of rental income of persons ranged between 2.5 and 3.5 percent of national income (Woytinsky 1967:135).

In 1963, 21 percent of the national income originated in corporate business. The other sector or private business (mutual financial institutions, cooperatives, nonprofit organizations, individually owned property, etc.) generated about seven percent of the national income. Income originating in general government (compensation of employees grew more substantially, from an average of 4.9 percent of national income during the 1920s to almost 13 percent during the 1960s (Woytinsky 1967:136).

In terms of industrial origin, there were changes in the relative importance of different sectors of the economy in production of national income. The share of agriculture (including forestry and fisheries) fluctuated around four percent, accounting for $20 billion out of about $555 billion in 1965. The share of mining also fell. Mining output contributed only $5-$6 billion or 1.2 percent in the 1960s. Manufacturing's share in national income amounted to 30 percent in 1964. The overall share of industries declined from 46 percent in 1950 to about 40 percent in 1964. Services, including government, maintained their share of about 55-60 percent of national income throughout most of this period, with slight ups and downs. Within this broad group, there were considerable changes: the share of transportation declined from 7.5 percent in 1929 to four percent in the 1960s; that of government increased from six percent in 1929 to about 13-14 percent in the 1960s (Woytinsky 1967:136-137).

Total personal income exceeded $400 billion in 1960 and reached $536 billion in the third quarter of 1965. Per capita personal income for the entire nation increased from $2,215 in 1960 to $2,724 in 1965. The growth of per capita personal income by 23 percent between 1960 and 1965 was the result of an increase in real purchasing power, since consumer prices were advancing during this period by about 1.5 percent a year. However, there was a wide interstate variation in the level of per capita personal income in 1964, ranging from $1,438 in Mississippi to $3,460 in Delaware and $3,544 in the District of Columbia. Nine states reported per capita personal incomes above $3,000; 12 reported incomes ranging from $2,500 to $3,000; and 11 states, incomes under $2,000. By 1965, only five states were in this last income group (Woytinsky 1967:141-142).

The number of consumer units (families and unattached individuals) increased from 48.8 million in 1950 to 57.9 million in 1962. The aggregate family personal income (before taxes) rose from $217.3 billion in 1950 to $420.4 billion in 1962. Average personal income per consumer unit rose from $4,440 in 1950 to $7,510 in 1963. In 1962, there were 46.9 million families and 11 million unattached individuals in the United States. The average family personal income increased from $6,303 in 1955 to $8,151 in 1962; that of unattached individuals, from $2,663 in 1955 to $3,472 in 1962. The average number of persons per family was 3.6 in 1955 and 3.7 in 1962. Their per capita family personal incomes were $1,755 in 1955 and $2,211 in 1962 (Woytinsky 1967:142-143).

Although economic progress was being achieved, inequality in income and contrasts between wealth and poverty persisted in the United States. First of all, there was almost complete stability in the relative distribution of family personal income from 1947 to 1962. The lowest fifth of the families and unattached individuals received only 4.6 percent of the total personal income in 1962; the highest quintal received 45.5 percent. Furthermore, the top five percent of consumer units accounted for 19.6 percent of all units (Woytinsky 1967:144-145). In short, very small gains were made in the redistribution of national income, and at the bottom of the income scale was still a substantial proportion of consumer units.

In 1962, the aggregate personal income of the lowest fifth of consumer units was 4.6 percent before tax and 4.9 percent after payment of the tax. However, the share of the highest fifth, who pay a progressively higher income tax, declined from 45.5 percent before the tax to 43.7 percent after the tax. The corresponding figures for the top five percent of the consumer units were 19.6 percent before and 17.7 percent after. Among the 57.9 million consumer units in 1962, 4.3 million were farm-operator families and 11 million were unattached individuals. The two groups were heavily represented in the income bracket under $30,000: 1.7 and 5.7 million, respectively. The lowest fifth of income recipients included some retired persons who lived independently and supplemented their social security benefits—and, in certain cases, their accumulated savings—by small current income. These individuals, however, were not necessarily people of low-income status (Woytinsky 1967:146).

The 1960 census revealed contrasts in the distribution of 45.1 million families in terms of income size by race and the type of area in which they lived. While almost one-half of all white families had incomes above $6,000, less than one-fifth of all nonwhite families had such incomes. Median income of white families ranged from $5,200 in the South to $6,700 in the West; the corresponding figures for nonwhite families ranged from $2,600 in the South to $5,400 in the West. The median income of urban families was $6,166; of rural non-farm families, $4,750; and of rural farm families, $3,228. Of the 4.1 million boys aged 14-19 years, seven out of 10 reported earning less than $1,000; nearly one in four earned $1,000-$2,999; and the remainder earned incomes exceeding $3,000. For those 20-24 years old, about one in six earned less than $1,000; two out of five earned under $3,000; somewhat more than one in 20 earned more than $6,000 (Woytinsky 1967:147).

Although total disposable income more than quintupled (in current dollars) between 1929 and 1964, the increase in per capita disposable income was quite negligible due to the population growth. Between 1950 and 1964, per capita income increased by less than 30 percent. However, between 1946–1949 and 1963, net personal savings grew from $9.8 billion to $27.5 billion, despite the simultaneous growth of debts to corporations and financial intermediaries from $9.8 billion to $35.5 billion (Woytinsky 1967:148–149).

While these figures may look impressive, a less cheerful picture emerges when one looks at how assets were distributed among American families. About one-third of the families (35 percent) had no liquid assets (US savings bonds, checking and savings accounts in banks, and shares in savings and loan associations and credit unions; currency is excluded) at all in 1964; 15 percent had less than $500 each; and 32 percent owned from $500 to $2,499. On the opposite end of the scale, 12 percent of the families possessed from $5,000 to $24,999, and one percent owned $25,000 or more (Woytinsky 1967:151–153).

In terms of individual debts, short- and intermediate-term consumer credits (installment credit, charge accounts, single-payment loans, etc.) multiplied about tenfold between 1929 and 1964, from $7.1 billion to $76.7 billion. Of these debts, installment credit saw the greatest increase. In 1929, both installment and non-installment credits were almost equal in size: $3.5 billion and $3.6 billion, respectively. In 1964, the corresponding figures were $59.3 billion and $17.4 billion. The most important single item of installment credit was automobile paper (Woytinsky 1967:153).

California and New York (the two largest states in the Union) combined received almost one-fourth of all personal income in the 1960s. Along with Illinois, Pennsylvania, Ohio, Texas, Michigan, New Jersey, Massachusetts, and Florida, they accounted for six-tenths of the total. At the other end of the spectrum, the whole group of 21 states lowest in personal income (each with less than $4 billion) had considerably less than either California or New York (Woytinsky 1967:154–155).

In sum, the affluence of the early to mid 1960s was conducive to promoting the altruistic movement of that era. For a time, the unprecedented economic growth of the period was favorable to political activists. The New Economic Policy demonstrated that purposeful government can make a difference. This altruism also coincided with a vibrant upswing in the business cycle and with the movement of thousands of citizens into the middle classes. But this affluence also was a mixed blessing: by affecting so many people, it also prompted unrealistic expectations. The poor, African Americans, and other ethnic groups, though better off than ever before, learned from modern communications (especially television) how much they were lacking. In fact, the gap between incomes of African Americans and those of whites widened. Income disparities between states were also enormous. While Northeastern and far Western states enjoyed unprecedented prosperity, the South and Southeastern states remained relatively poor.

Social Environment

Three major social issues dominated the American landscape from the early to mid-1960s. These issues included poverty, peace movement, and black power movement. Together, these three issues revealed the flaws of endless growth and the dangers in the assumptions that underlie it. Toward the end of the 1960s, genuine crisis threatened.

Poverty

The American government made major efforts to deal with poverty during the 1960s. The Economic Opportunity Act of 1964 encompassed a series of programs ranging from Job Corps and Head Start to Community Action programs and loans to small businesses in poverty areas. After the government had spent billions of dollars on these programs, it was obvious by the end of the 1960s that the programs were not the major success many had hoped they would be.

However, President Kennedy was credited with the first major effort to alleviate poverty in America. Among his strategies was a series of tax reductions which were aimed at giving a break to the poor. Arthur Schlesinger believed that the tax reductions had to be expanded, "by a comprehensive structural counterpart taking the form, not of piecemeal programs, but a broad war against poverty itself." This approach, he believed, would pull a host of social programs together and rally the country behind a noble cause (Johnson 1965:1008).

Other efforts included the expansion of social security and welfare payments, medical assistance for the aged, and efforts by those in the business sector to train and employ those previously left out. Yet, there were still over 20 million Americans who were poor by definition, and millions more not far above the poverty line (Lillibridge 1976:301).

In addition to the relative failure of the "war against poverty," wealth was not being put to the best use. Too much was being spent on personal and private use. Although a greater majority of Americans than ever before were enjoying the material good life, fewer resources were available to improve the quality of life in the broader social arena. As a result, a whole set of problems began to get out of hand. For example, the nation faced a crime problem of major proportion. Fifty percent of arrests were of persons under 24, many of them blacks, indicating that society was neglecting both its young and its largest racial minority. Many Americans cited the breakdown of "law and order" as the reason for the problem. Thus, these individuals suggested that the problem could be solved by beefing up the police and strengthening the courts. Large sums were spent on these suggestions, but no significant results were achieved (Lillibridge 1976:302).

In the area of health, billions of dollars were also poured into medical research, by now the best in the world. But, the gains were not quite significant either. With the absence of a national health insurance program, medical personnel greatly increased, while hospital and clinical facilities never got a fair share of the national wealth. The ironic consequence was that while America could accomplish one heart transplant after another, it was behind Yugoslavia and 15 other countries in its capacity to save the lives of newborn infants (Lillibridge 1976:302).

Another major problem was the decay of American cities. The government attempted to promote urban renewal and eliminate urban blight through the Model Cities program, housing development, and other programs, but the results were disappointing. While few cities such as Boston, New Haven, and Philadelphia managed to rebuild central areas, the total effect was negligible. Expenditures on private satisfaction led to clogged streets and highways with automobiles while public transportation languished. Passenger trains nearly disappeared, bus and subway services crumbled, while $33 billion was spent on the construction of an elaborate interstate highway system to satisfy private and certain business interests (Lillibridge 1976:302). Francis Nichol, Chairman of the French Department of the District of Columbia Public Schools System, interviewed for this book on July 29, 1992, summarized the problem quite well when he stated that "At the heart of the dilemma of the 1960s was that while many Americans took pleasure in consuming, few took pleasure in producing."

Peace Movement
The peace movement of the 1960s will be remembered more for raising

America's social conscience on the tragedies of wars, not for its ability to unify its various constituencies. Three factors made it difficult to unify the various groups within the peace movement. First, the relationships between peace groups were carnivorous. Second, the strategy of the movement divided those who sought nuclear control from unilateralists, absolute pacifists, and sympathizers of the Viet Cong. Finally, the most serious problem was ideological, between those who accepted the Vietnam War as a political fact and those who viewed it as evidence of America's cultural exhaustion (Berman 1968:164).

The American peace movement varied a great deal. It ranged from established organizations like the American Friends Service Committee (AFSC) and the Women's International League for Peace and Freedom (WILPF), to the Vietnam Day Committee (VDC). It was divided by religion, policy, and social status. Because of this, amalgamating the various interests became its central problem. The case of SANE typifies the difficulties in coalescing the peace groups. SANE was formed by the union of pacifists and federalists. Although it held a moral position, it was unable to win support of noted experts in international affairs (Berman 1968:165).

With the passage of time, the problem became magnified. The demonstrations at Berkeley in 1965 were followed by some abusive behaviors of men like Robert Pickus, who suggested that the peace movement rid itself of those attached to totalitarian politics (Berman 1968:165).

The first of the peace movement's great problems emerged when it tried to create a common ground for Quakers, pacifists, unilateralists, federalists, and those who were interested simply in issues of testing or shelters. The second was the permeability of the movement to Communism. The third had to do with the split once again between the community of interests during the mid-1960s—the divergence between democratic and nondemocratic pacifism (Berman 1968:165–166).

Black Power Movement

When the sit-ins first attracted national attention in 1960, the civil rights movement served as the vanguard for domestic reform. The movement sustained the idealism that assisted broader movements for change by providing a cause worthy of sacrifice. However, as early as 1963, internal divisions began to split the interracial coalition. Widespread disruption and disillusion resulted in 1966 because of this disintegration. A major source for the discord was the militants' awareness of the limits of legal action in combating racial discrimination in the South. By 1964, more African American children were attending segregated schools in the Deep South than in 1954, the year of the supposedly epochal *Brown v Board of Education* decision. Jim Crow laws flourished throughout the South; African Americans and many poor whites still were denied the vote. The Civil Rights Acts of 1954 and 1964 rectified some of the injustices, but they came too late for activists (Patterson 1976:450).

The most divisive issue among the civil rights workers was the one about leadership. Militants argued that only African Americans could understand their own experiences and, thus, must lead the movement. Whites, on the other hand, argued that such an attempt was incompatible with the larger goal of the movement, since it appeared ethnocentric. Consequently, this issue prevented successful interracial drives for civil rights in the South after 1965 (Patterson 1976:450).

Militant African Americans came to distrust "paternalistic" white liberals as much as segregationists. The ultimate result was racial violence in northern cities. From 1964 to 1967, more than 200 people were killed and property worth over $200 million was destroyed during the riots (Patterson 1976:453).

Cultural Environment

Discussion of the American cultural environment during the early to mid-1960s usually centers on two topics: the consumer culture and the counter-culture that followed it. This approach results from the fact that the affluence of the era made possible a spectacular "culture boom" which gratified some citizens, but apparently depressed others.

Consumer Culture

The pacesetters for much of the popular culture—American teenagers—spent a staggering $22 billion in 1963 alone for goods that conformed to their tastes. They bought a wide variety of goods ranging from surfboards and transistor radios to *Glamour* and *Seventeen* (magazines) and, of course, millions of pop records (Leuchtenburg 1973:65).

Television exploded during this period like a time bomb. About 94 percent of American households owned at least one television set and millions possessed more than one (Leuchtenburg 1973:65). The television explosion meant that more goods and services could be sold through "slick" advertisements.

At the same time, however, the consumer culture underwent the most relentless criticism it had ever experienced. Critics noted that the value system of the consumer society was antihuman, a way of getting people to buy things they did not need. The play *Hair* mocked the consumer who pasted King Korn trading stamps in books one by one, and hippies rebelled against the "moneytheism" of an acquisitive society (Leuchtenburg 1973:186). This movement came to be known as the counterculture.

Counterculture

The overlapping of radical protests and rebellion against the lifestyles and values of the 1950s and early 1960s led to the unprecedented visibility received by the counterculture movement. A very large number of young men (and some adults) let their hair grow long, donned love beads, and dressed in faded jeans, work shirts, and sandals. An equally large number of young women (and some adults) walked about without bras or shoes and talked about sexual freedom. Many took marijuana or other more dangerous drugs, and lived in rural communes or in seedy urban areas like San Francisco's Haight-Asbury District. The very sight of such apparently unkempt people was offensive to many traditionalists (Patterson 1976:467).

The more staid Americans were also alarmed by the taste in popular music that appeared to addict many young people of the 1960s. Earlier in the decade, idealistic youth flocked to listen to folk musicians like Bob Dylan, Malvina Reynolds, and Joan Baez sing gentle lyrics of social protest. By the mid-1960s, however, many turned away from songs of social protests to those of rock groups like the Beatles, which contained only vague and tardy social messages. Many ambitious singers also concentrated on achieving a louder sound and more insistent beat. In addition, the Vietnam War induced growing anger and despair among the youth (Patterson 1976:467–468).

There was much more to the counterculture movement than just love beads and rock concerts. True believers questioned the existing values. They believed that their "revolution" was cultural and generational. Thus, they called for young people to transcend the old culture and advance to new thresholds of freedom. Central to the ideas of the true believers was the notion that the older generation was repressed. Surmounting repression for them meant rejecting taboos about sex. If sex was one avenue to transcendence, they reasoned, rejection of science was another. In this way, the foes of the old culture joined others in the 1960s who were vehemently opposed to materialism (Patterson 1976:469–470).

To replace material values, leaders of the counterculture called for a return to spiritualism. Human beings, they argued, must seek harmony with, not victory over, the natural world. Such faith in nature led to a movement for ecology, which appealed to thousands of Americans who otherwise had little use for the counterculture (Patterson 1976:470).

By the end of the decade, sharp differences between its members divided the youth movement. While many held vaguely New Left views on social issues, they were essentially nonpolitical. Their primary grievance was with adult culture, not with capitalism. New Lefts and black power advocates, accordingly, accused other groups within the movement ("flower children") of trying to cop out of society, instead of fighting it (Patterson 1976:470).

The preceding discussion deals with the first major research question of this book: In what type of political, economic, social, and cultural environment did the debate on bilingual education emerge? In sum, the American environment of the early to mid-1960s simply revealed the exhaustion of liberal culture. It also introduced into the American culture the imperatives of a movement hostile to liberalism. The interrelationship between this environment and the inputs should be so tight that it allows little or no dichotomy between the two in terms of the analysis that is to follow.

Chapter 3

INPUTS

The focus of this chapter is on the inputs—that is, demands and support—that caused changes in the environment relevant to the political system that led to the passage of the Bilingual Education Act of 1968. Specifically, attention is directed at (1) how the volume and variety of demands were regulated by certain structures—interest groups and opinion leaders—that aggregated and articulated the demands made on decisionmakers; (2) how support for the Act varied independently and how strong associative relationships emerged.

Unfortunately, not much data exist on either open or behind-the-scene demands and support that led to the Act. One reason for this, as revealed during the interviews conducted for this book, is that most of the actors are deceased and the others are no longer working for the United States government or the organizations that were involved. As Dr. E. Cubillios, Director of United States English (USE), stated during an interview, "I was in college when the 1968 Bilingual Education Act was being debated. As a matter of fact, I ended up being a beneficiary of the Act through the receipt of a fellowship that financed my college education." Another reason is that those organizations which today champion (e.g., National Clearinghouse on Bilingual Educaton—NACBE) or oppose (e.g., USE) the bilingual education program had not been formed prior to the 1968 Bilingual Education Act.

The Supreme Court

The United States Supreme Court ruled in the 1954 *Brown v Board of Education* case that school segregation based on race was unconstitutional. Although the Court did not specifically mention Hispanics or other ethnic minorities, the ruling stated that it applied to "others similarly situated." While this ruling did not directly affect the education of non-English speaking minorities, it did introduce a new era in American civil rights and led the way to subsequent legislation that would create programs for the disadvantaged (NACBE 1988:1). As discussions in chapters four and five reveal, the *Brown* ruling was widely cited by many demand articulators as justification for bilingual education programs during the debate over the 1968 Act.

The Civil Rights Movement

During the 1960s, African Americans and other minority groups held demonstrations to protest underemployment, inadequate housing, poor representation in government, and lack of educational opportunity. The social climate (see details in chapter four) clearly dictated that action must be taken to rectify these inequalities. In 1964, the 88th Congress passed the Civil Rights Act which defined the concept of equality in federal law. Several parts of this Act were relevant to language minority students. For instance, Title IV of the Act stipulated that the Attorney General could initiate school desegregation suits if private citizens were unable to file suit effectively. Furthermore, Title VI of the Act stated that any person participating in any program receiving federal financial aid could not be discriminated against on the basis of race or national origin (NACBE 1988:1). For those who would fail to comply with the law, federal agencies were charged with the responsibility of imposing sanctions against them. These sanctions included withdrawal of federal subsidies, an important sanction since many educational institutions relied heavily on federal assistance (NACBE 1988:1–2).

Indeed, the legislative branch (like the executive and the judiciary branches) was influenced by the demand articulators of the civil rights movement, because they (demand articulators) focused on the deprivations suffered by various minority groups. Consequently, the wave of ethnic consciousness, which accompanied the civil rights movement and social changes in the 1960s, encouraged Spanish-speaking parents and community leaders to loudly express their desire that the Spanish language be given a more meaningful role in their children's education.

Local Boards of Education

The input of local boards of education to the debate over the 1968 Bilingual Education Act comprised three major studies. The first was the 1958 New York City Board of Education *Puerto Rican Study*. This was a comprehensive study dealing with the difficulties encountered by native Spanish-speaking students in the New York school system. The second was a study conducted by the Texas Education Agency in 1965 on the problems of Spanish-surnamed students in the Texas school system. The third was the 1967 Colorado study of the status of the Spanish-surnamed population in the state (Leibowitz 1980:11). Together, these studies made it very clear to members of Congress that education was one of the major issues of the Spanish-speaking population.

The Executive Branch

The executive branch, through its Department of Health, Education and Welfare (HEW), and Department of Interior, focused exclusively on the educational needs of Native American children. To a certain degree, this need was linked to additional control being transferred by the federal government to Native Americans with respect to curriculum and school staffing. The official position of the executive branch was not very supportive of the push for the Bilingual Education Act. While it agreed that the educational benefits of bilingual education were desirable, the executive branch argued that implementing such a program would be quite difficult (Leibowitz 1980:11).

Hispanic Advocacy Groups

Before the passage of the 1968 Bilingual Education Act, no well-organized advocacy group was in existence. For example, the Mexican American Defense Fund (MADF) was founded in 1989, USE was inaugurated in 1982, NACBE was established in 1975.

The Hispanic advocacy groups that existed before the passage of the Act were made up of loose coalitions of parents and community leaders. Although these groups were generally concerned with civil rights issues by 1968, they apparently had not concentrated on bilingual education issues before the

Act's passage led to their mobilization in support of the programs. During the hearings, the leaders of these Hispanic advocacy groups repeatedly indicated that the Bilingual Education Act was a necessary first step in promoting full participation by linguistic minorities in America's economic, political, and social life. Citing their children's low achievement scores and high dropout rates, they argued that Hispanics in particular had suffered consistent disadvantages in the educational process. Educational failure in turn, they reasoned, prevented Hispanics from obtaining higher-status jobs and gaining political access. Improved education, they concluded, could impede this pattern of limited life chances (Moran 1988:1260–1261).

However, there was disagreement between Hispanic parents and community leaders in terms of how best to accomplish their educational objectives. At the hearings, many community leaders mistakenly assumed that the Act would restrict the instructional options available to state and local educators. As a result, they focused on which options the federal government should sponsor. Since these community leaders believed that English-only curriculum impeded non-english proficient (NEP) and limited English proficient (LEP) students' performance, they called for bilingual education programs that would eliminate linguistic and cultural barriers to achievement. In addition, they contended that instruction that was sensitive to cultural heritage could enrich the educational experience of all Hispanic students, no matter what their linguistic background (Moran 1988:1261).

Some parents and community leaders called for linguistic and cultural diversity through multilingual, multicultural curricula. They wanted to promote bilingualism and biculturalism for all students, rather than Hispanic or linguistic minority students alone (Moran 1988:1261). In such a vein, bilingual education would not be conceptualized as compensatory or remedial instruction. Instead, it would be seen as a useful skill that could benefit a student. Some even posited that general improvement in the nation's linguistic competencies and tolerance for other cultures could greatly improve the United States' international relations with other countries, especially those in Latin America (Moran 1988:1262).

Education Experts

Education experts largely agreed with Hispanic advocacy groups on the issue that Hispanics had suffered a tragic history of educational failure. However, some of them reached quite different conclusions from this history. They opined that Hispanics' low achievement scores and high attrition rates reflected the need for compensatory programs that would integrate Hispanics more effectively into the mainstream of American education. These experts called, therefore, for bilingual education as a way of promoting assimilation through the acquisition of English (Moran 1988:1262).

Other education experts raised questions about the effectiveness of bilingual education in dealing with LEP and NEP students' academic problems. They also raised concerns about how the programs would be implemented. At the hearings, these education experts, small in number, were overwhelmed by Hispanic advocates who touted bilingual education as a panacea for Hispanic students' educational dilemmas (Moran 1988:1262–1263).

It is obvious from the preceding discussion that the demands made on and support received by members of Congress from different articulators did influence the outcome of the 1968 Bilingual Education Act. As chapter four shows, the Act left program objectives vague, an indication that its passage required hard political compromise. While Hispanic parents and community leaders had hoped for a federal mandate for bilingual education programs, what they got was an Act that established only a modest grant-in-aid program to support experimental demonstration projects. Moreover, the Act represented a minimal intrusion on state and local policy makers' prerogatives by not stipulating that they design special programs for LEP and NEP students.

Subsystem Components: Legislative Processes

Legislative political processes will not be complete without the role and inputs of the subsystems. These include interest groups, political parties, press, experts, and/or any other category of people interested and/or affected by the bilingual education legislation. These groups include, but are not limited to, the National Education Association (NEA); United States Catholic Conference (USCC); American Council on Education (ACE); National Congress of Parents and Teachers (NCPT); the AFL-CIO Executive Council; Citizens for Educational Freedom (CEF); Agudath Israel of America Organization (AIAO); American Federation of Teachers (AFT); AFL-CIO; James E. Allen, Jr., Commissioner of Education, New York State; Dr. Ralph

Dillard, Superintendent of San Diego City Schools; Dr. Sidney P. Marland, Jr., Superintendent of Public Schools, Pittsburgh; Dr. Bernard E. Donovan, Superintendent of New York City Public Schools; Dr. Melvin W. Barnes, Superintendent of Schools, San Francisco; Richard H. Goodman, Executive Secretary New England School Development Council; Robert H. Marden, Director, BRIDGE Project of New England School Development Council, Cambridge, Massachusetts; Dr. Theodore R. Sizer, Dean, Harvard Graduate School of Education; Dr. William H. Ohrenberger, Superintendent of Public Schools, Boston; Dr. John B. Davis, Jr., Superintendent of Schools, Minneapolis; Dr. Richardson Dilworth, President, the Board of Education of Philadelphia; Dr. Joseph Manch, Superintendent of Schools, Buffalo, New York; Dr. James A. Hazlett, Superintendent of Schools, Kansas City, Missouri; Dr. E.C. Stimbert, Superintendent of Schools, Memphis, Tennessee; Dr. Robert B. French, Superintendent of Schools, Dayton, Ohio; Ernest Stapleton, Assistant Superintendent of Schools, Albuquerque, New Mexico; Fred Breit, Deputy Superintendent of Schools, Seattle, Washington; Hugh Calkins, Member of Cleveland School Board; E. Craig Brandenberg, General Secretary, Board of Christian Education, Evangelical United Brethren Church; Charman Hunter, Director, Department of Christian Education, Episcopal Church; Charles K. Johnson, Secretary General, Division of Parish Education, United Church of Christ; Carroll Johnson, Superintendent of Schools, White Plains, New York; Charles Holt, Superintendent of Schools, South Bend, Indiana; Elizabeth Koontz, President, Department of Classroom Teachers, National Education Association; and John M. Lumley, Director, Division of Federal Relations, National Education Associations.

These actors along with the press and political parties articulated demands and/or support during the debate and the hearings on bilingual education programs. Consequently, the Bilingual Education Act that was enacted on January 2, 1968, included P.L. 90-247, Title VII, Section 702 under the umbrella of the Elementary and Secondary Education Act of 1965 (H.R. 7819).

The Hearing Testimonies

Most of the testimonies during the hearing and debate on bilingual education, as stated before, centered on praise and support for the programs.

Nothing was in the hearing that typically represents what one might refer to as demand articulation. There was a tremendous struggle over federal versus state control over the funds for bilingual education and other purposes. One of the most serious oppositions was registered by Senator Thurmond, one of the three senators who voted against the bill. In his words,

> Mr. President, there are good things and bad things in this bill as it has been reported by the Conference Committee.... It would be unwise for the Senate to pass this legislation. Let me summarize my reasons. First, I have always felt that it was a mistake for the Federal Government to get into the field of education because coercion and control would inevitably follow. I am not inclined to vote for a general education bill so long as coercion and pressure over and beyond statutory requirement occurs. This coercion above and beyond the law continues to this day. Second, I believe that this is a very large expenditure for Congress to authorize at a time of inflationary pressure on the economy this bill authorizes over 9.2 billion, which I believe to be unnecessary at this time (US Congress 1967:37036-37037).

Besides voting against the bill, Senator Thurmond offered an amendment to the bill which was to prevent the "ever increasing trend toward federal control of education" (US Congress 1967:37037).

As expected, Senator Yarborough spoke at length in favor of the bill and went on to explain the true significance of the bill to the nation in general and, Texas, his home state, in particular. He also joined his colleagues in paying tribute to all those who participated favorably in the "dance of legislation." Parts of Yarborough's speech read as follows:

> Mr. President, the Conference Report on the Elementary and Secondary Education Act represents the joint efforts by many people of this nation to give increased opportunity to the more than 50 million school-age children in the United States. Almost 3 million of these children live in my home state of Texas. I am proud to support this major bill which will increase the opportunities for the disadvantaged children, as well as raise the general quality of education in this country. For the State of Texas, the bill has special meaning; for we have long lagged behind in education despite the wealth of our State. Nonetheless, when measured against the low per-capita income level of our state, the comparable effort which is being made by us is among the highest in the nation. Under the incentive provision of this bill, Texas receives almost $4 million to be utilized under Title I grants.... Under the regular provision of Title I, Texas will receive almost $78 million.
>
> ...The amendment to provide technical assistance to rural areas is especially important to my state, since we have many small local school districts without money, personnel, or expertise to even fill out the forms to qualify for programs of

Federal aid. This amendment provides additional money to my dissemination of information amendment of last year to assist schools.... Finally, this bill contains a major new title, the Bilingual Education Act. I introduced the bill (S.428) on January 17 of this year, after having been to a couple of conferences in the Southwest on this problem.

...The problem is that many of our school-age children come from homes where the mother tongue is not English. As a result, these children enter school not speaking English and not able to understand the instructions that is all conducted in English. In my own State of Texas and indeed in the entire Southeast, this is not an isolated problem, but one which involves millions of school children.

In Texas, the years of school completed for those who are white is 10.8 years, for non-whites 8.1 years, but only 4.7 years, for the Spanish surnamed. Over one-half of the Spanish surnamed families have incomes under the poverty level of $3,000, and 13.6 percent have incomes under $1,000 in Texas. To alleviate this problem, I introduced S.428 to provide Federal assistance to local school districts in establishing and operating bilingual programs to create a more feasible transition into our schools for these children by giving them special educational programs aimed at solving their problems.

Our hearings received broad testimony as to the urgent need for this legislation to provide equal educational opportunity for those children who do not come to school with English-speaking ability. We received almost unanimous enthusiasm and support for this legislation as being an effective remedial program (US Congress 1967:37037).

According to Senator Yarborough's speech, therefore, there were factors other than pressure or interest groups that affected the passage of the 1968 Bilingual Education Act. The press, as always, plays its role in providing news and information to the public, including the Congress. Several times during the hearings and debate many senators prefaced their questions or remarks by referring to an article or a publication in a major newspaper, for example. During the House hearings, Mr. Anderson, a congressman from Illinois questioning Mr. Howe, started by saying "My attention has been called to an article in the *New York Times* a few days ago," and Congressman Mill similarly followed by "Also in today's *Washington Evening Star*... and I ask unanimous consent that the two articles to which I have referred be printed in the record" (US Congress 1967:13327). This is quite indicative of the fact that albeit members of the press are not interest groups per se, they aid in the process of demand and support articulation by providing vital information to Congress, upon which sometimes their policy decisions are based.

During the hearings, the testimonies, as indicated earlier, were centered on jurisdictional as opposed to substantive issues on the one hand and method of disbursement on the other. The question that one congressman asked was the following: "What is the proper relationship between State and local government on the one hand, and the national government on the other?" (US Congress 1977:3326). Further testimonies were on the appropriateness of block grants on the one hand and formula grants on the other. Educators who testified before the Committee on Education and Labor were overwhelmingly in favor of the block grant approach. To this effect, Albert Quie introduced an amendment popularly known as the Quie Amendment. He insisted that "all this money comes from home: now we ought to send some of it back without strings attached" (US Congress 1977:13327). On the other hand, the United States Catholic Conference (USCC) and other private schools were more concerned about the rights of children in private schools under this legislation.

There was an ideological divide among the parties and factions involved. The Republicans and others favoring federal control were more in support of the formula grant. The Democrats and those in favor of state and local control favored the block grant approach. The testimonies could be summarized in this manner: block grants will allow local governments to do as they please while formula grants will allow the mighty hands of national government to dictate. Prior to the enactment of H.R. 7819, the entire education programs were under the Higher Education Act. The debate on education had been ongoing in the 1960s. The bilingual education legislation was, therefore, an amendment to the Elementary and Secondary Education Act that appropriated funds for the education of language-minority children and other purposes. Unlike many other bills, it was a bipartisan effort that brought about this expanded policy. However, there was still some disagreement between the two parties on the modalities of this impending legislation. The Democrats were more supportive than the Republicans and some in fact thought that the Great Society Program of President Johnson had gone too far. Former President Gerald R. Ford, in his address to the House on December 13, 1967, charged that

the Great Society Program of Lyndon Johnson has become a runaway locomotive with a wild-eyed engineer at the throttle. The American people can be thankful that the 90th Congress has slowed down this locomotive which is hurtling down the track toward national bankruptcy.... The man in the White House can only be described as wild when he continues to talk about greater and greater spending on social welfare schemes...." (US Congress 1967:3628).

As indicated earlier, the Bilingual Education Act received bipartisan support and was introduced simultaneously in the House and the Senate. The Senate bill was introduced by a ranking member, Senator Ralph Yarborough of Texas. He later became the Chairman of the Senate Committee on Labor and Public Welfare in 1969. His standing in the Senate was particularly important because it directly impacted the fate of the bill. According to Walter Oleszek (1978:66), one way of ensuring that a bill receives committee attention is to have it introduced by a high-ranking member of the House or Senate. This was the case in the bilingual education legislation. Due to the collegial nature of Congress, there is the tendency for members to compromise and negotiate rather than oppose one another outright. Senator Yarborough limited his bill to Spanish-speaking by birth only partly because his home state was to benefit by this limitation.

In the House of Representatives, the bills advocating bilingual education were introduced by Congressman Augustus Hawkins, Chairman of the House Education and Labor Committee, Edward Royball of California, and Congressman Jerome Scheur of New York. The Hawkins-Royball bill added French-speaking to the Senate bill and the Scheur bill authorized bilingual education for all children whose native tongues were other than English.

Political Parties and Bureaucracy

In the case of the bilingual education bill, the role of the parties and other groups were highly diminished due to the nature of the legislation. For once, the proposed bill had support of both political parties because it was non-controversial. The support from both parties was in principle. But, some Republicans were concerned about the growing national deficit which was at this time estimated at $35 billion (US Congress 1967:36328). Although it is not abnormal for Congress to provide authorization for programs without appropriation, the delay in the case of the Bilingual Education Act was intentional. As noted in chapter one, the funding for these programs under Title VII did not materialize until the following year (1969). Most of the debate and testimonies that ensued on this bill were centered around how the funds were to be dispensed. Other aspects were more symbolic than substantive as captured by Larry Wade when he noted that

> Politics is more than a struggle over the distribution of material values. It is also a social process through which symbolic values representing the need for self-esteem—personal rectitude—are distributed and validated. Symbolic purpose may be adequately accomplished through granting formal recognition in the preamble of legislation. Furthermore, there may be no political support turning symbolic victories into material accomplishments (1972:22).

In addition, the ideological differences between the two political parties played a major role in the debate over the details of the Bilingual Education Act. Ideological differences have historically separated the Republican and Democratic parties since the beginning of the American Republic. These unique differences were captured by the McClonsky research teams in their study of party leaders and their partisan voters. They found and asserted the following:

> Democratic leaders typically display the urge to elevate the low born, the uneducated, the deprived minorities and the poor in general; they are also more disposed to employ the Nation's collective power to advance humanitarian and social goals (e.g., social security, immigration, racial integration, a higher minimum wage, and public education).... The Democrats are more progressively-oriented toward social reform and experimentation. The Republican leaders, while not uniformly different from their opponents, subscribe in greater measure to the symbol and practice of individualism, *laissez-faire*.... They prefer to overcome humanity's misfortunes by relying on personal efforts, private incentives, frugality, hard work, responsibility, self-denial (both for men and government), and the strengthening rather than the diminution of the economic status that are the 'natural' rewards of the differences in human character and fortunes (McClonsky et al 1963:56).

Based on the preceding analysis, it is no surprise that bilingual education is a Democratic issue and was introduced under the leadership of Lyndon Johnson.

The diminished role of political parties in bilingual education programs tends to support the thesis advanced in political science by some scholars that political parties are in decline. These scholars include, but are not limited to, William Crotty and Garry Jacobson (1980). By looking at recent developments in campaign politics, they found that the influence of political parties has declined significantly, and that party organizations now play diminished roles. This observation by no means announces the obituary for modern political parties. They remain resilient and continue to serve as the linkage organization between the electorate and the government. The longevity of the

American political party dates back as far as the 1800s; the first in the world, followed by Britain 17 years later (Ladd 1970). Political parties, albeit a victim of high-tech campaign and politics, have continued to withstand the test of time and have remained a dominant political institution in America.

Similar to political parties, the bureaucracy also played a limited role in the passage of the Bilingual Education Act. However, this is not attributed to a diminished capacity. As a matter of fact, the new trend has shown increased administrative influence. According to Francis Rourke,

> a growing reliance on the skills of bureaucrats in the operation of modern government has been coupled with general distrust of bureaucratic power. No aspect of the growth of bureaucratic power in this century has been more important than the steady expansion in the scope of administrative discretion (1976:50).

This administrative discretion, as defined by Rourke, constitutes the ability to choose among competing alternatives, that is, to determine how state powers are utilized in specific instances (1976:50). This concern is also shared by Randall Ripley and Grace Franklin (1980:2) in their discussion of administrative agenda setting. This includes national policy initiatives and the power to shape or alter public policies. The role of the bureaucracy in the case of the Bilingual Education Act was limited by the origin of the bill. Since the bill originated in Congress, and was in congruence with the general thrust of the Johnson Administration's policies, there was a limited role in bureaucratic action. However, various relevant agencies provided information inputs as discussed in the preceding chapter.

Interest Groups and Organizations
This analysis of the subsystem began with a list of several interest groups and organizations that provided inputs and articulated the competing positions in the environment. David Easton recognized the role of interest groups in formulating and articulating policies. They also provide valuable clues or information to legislators which they use to support their policy positions. They also monitor and contribute to the feedback mechanism. In terms of importance, they constitute a major source of education and information to Congress. One staff aide explained the following in Ornstein and Elder (1978:59):

> There are hundreds of things happening here at any given time, including committee hearings, roll call votes on the floor and meetings. Senators run from

meetings to hearings on the floor and back again all day long. There's not enough time to think and they need information in a condensed and easily digestible form. Staff provide some of this, but lobbyists are indispensable sources both to us and to Senators.

This important role of interest groups can, oftentimes, be detrimental to the policy process. This is because these groups represent special interest and, as such, could provide fragmented information to suit their purpose and protect or promote the interests of those they represent.

The role of these groups was also highly limited in the case of the Bilingual Education Act. As previously discussed, many of these groups that form the core of interest groups on both sides of the bilingual education debate were either nonexistent or informal. For example, the NACBE was founded in 1975, USE was founded in 1982, and the MADF was founded in 1989. Moreover, the literature on bilingual education suggest that the Bilingual Education Act did not attain national prominence until the Supreme Court decision was rendered in *Lau v Nichols*. Prior to *Lau*, the Act was not considered a major legislation and therefore did not attract much attention. An examination of the listing of major legislation passed in Congress between 1965 and 1968 did not include the Bilingual Education Act of 1968 (US Congress 1965-1968:719-733, 1968:34-41). Besides, the federal government created several agencies within the HEW to primarily monitor, articulate and, where necessary, take remedial action to protect and advance the rights of minorities. These agencies included, but were not limited to, the Office for Civil Rights, the Bureau of Indian Affairs, and the Bureau of Mexican Affairs. The United States Civil Rights Commission was also very influential and contributed to the passage of many laws, including the Bilingual Education Act.

The United States Commission on Civil Rights

The United States Commission on Civil Rights is an independent, bipartisan agency established by Congress in 1957 and charged with the following duties:

1. Investigate complaints alleging denial of the right to vote by reason of race, color, religion, sex, or national origin, or by reason of fraudulent practices.

2. Study and collect information concerning legal developments

constituting a denial of equal protection of the laws under the Constitution because of race, color, religion, sex, or national origin, or in the administration of justice.

3. Appraise federal laws and policies with respect to the denial of equal protection of the laws because of race, color, sex, religion, or national origin, or in the administration of justice.

4. Serve as a national clearinghouse for information concerning denials of equal protection of the laws because of race, color, religion, sex, or national origin.

5. Submit reports, findings, and recommendations to the President and Congress.

From time to time, the Commission acts as a watchdog for civil rights violations, and prepares reports for educators and the general public on diverse issues dealing with civil rights. The Commission was expected to play a major role in bilingual education legislation based on its functional description. However, the Bilingual Education Act was not viewed mainly as a civil rights law until the Supreme Court's ruling in *Lau v Nichols*. The United States Commission on Civil Rights issued several reports on civil rights issues including bilingual education. Similar to the political parties and interest groups, its major report entitled "A Better Chance to Learn: Bilingual-Bicultural Education" was not published until 1975, seven years after the passage of the Bilingual Education Act of 1968. In essence, its impact was also limited in terms of demand articulation and providing input to the legislative process that produced the Act under study.

The thrust of the arguments presented in this segment points to the fact that most of the present-day demand articulators were handicapped by circumstances and thus had limited impact on the bilingual education legislation of 1968. This point was further strengthened by Moran when she observed and noted that

...although Hispanic advocacy groups were generally concerned with civil rights issues by 1968, they apparently had not concentrated on bilingual education issues before the Act's passage precipitated their mobilization in support of the programs....The passage of the Bilingual Education Act in 1968 was prompted by (1) the arrival of a large number of non-English-speaking Cuban refugees after Fidel

Castro assumed power; (2) a growing awareness on the part of several Senators, especially Ralph Yarborough, of NEP and LEP students educational problems; and (3) the ongoing impact of the civil rights movement (Moran 1988:1260–1261).

Moran concluded that while Hispanics had become highly sensitized to civil rights issues, this evidence does not suggest that they pressed strongly for bilingual education reforms before 1968. Despite the fact that Senator Yarborough seems to have personal concern for LEP and NEP students, there was also the "desire to enhance his political stature and national visibility" (1988:1261). In that regard, the Senator was quite successful. This scenario is not only limited to the national level because studies in other states came in with similar findings. For example, in Texas, San Miguel Guadalupe found that while there was abundant support for bilingual education programs, some of the public proclamations of support were "aimed at gaining the political support of the growing Mexican vote in Texas" (1983:25).

The Bilingual Education Act of 1968 was not a controversial legislation, as mentioned earlier. At the introduction of the bill in the Senate, Yarborough had seven sponsors. The roll call vote was almost unanimous with 63 yeas, 3 nays, and 43 not voting. It was not only the proper thing to do at that time, it was the politically right thing to do. Note that this was the 89th Congress which President Johnson did not only call productive, but also called it "my own Congress."

This chapter focuses on the second major research question of this book: What were the positions of the competing factions that lobbied Congress on the issue of bilingual education and how can they be characterized? It is clear from the preceding discussion that these factions were not in opposition to the bill, but had some differences of opinion as to how to best serve the language-minority children. Many were just trying to cash in on the supportive political atmosphere that paved the way for a multitude of legislation passed under President Johnson's Great Society Program.

Chapter 4

LEGISLATIVE SYSTEM

This chapter explores what David Easton referred to as "the authoritative allocation of values for society" (1965a:49) in terms of the Bilingual Education Act of 1968. The roles played by members of the federal legislature and their pattern of interaction are examined. This exploration makes it possible to comprehend the processes of how binding decisions about the Act were made and implemented.

The Context for Political Action

As stated in preceding chapters, political leaders and educators decided to take action to abolish discrimination and lower the barriers to full participation in the 1960s. Their concern tended to focus on the approximately 10 million Mexican Americans and Native Americans. A new generation of leaders had come out of these two communities during the decade; many had gone to universities in Texas and California or had moved to the cities of the midwest, where they gained a sense of their own identities and keen perception of the educational and economic problems facing Mexican Americans and Native Americans. Some ran for public office or started student, social, and labor movements which raised the consciousness of many Americans about their plight (Garcia 1974). A new set of leaders and ideas also came from overseas. The post-World War II immigrations of intellectuals and professionals from Eastern Europe, the Mediterranean, and Asia awakened other Americans to the value of the languages and cultures of their ancestral homelands. They also heard about the worldwide resurgence of interest in ethnic identities. As a result of all these forces, a new generation of Americans expressed a desire to learn the languages abandoned by their immigrant grandparents and rejected by their parents.

Without the civil rights movement, however, calls for new policies concerning language could have been ignored. The Supreme Court's decision of 1954 banning segregated schools opened a new chapter in American history. From then on during the late 1950s and 1960s, African American–led organizations pressed for changes in education, voting and housing restrictions, and discriminatory employment practices. The numerous laws passed, speeches by leaders of all races and religions, orders by Presidents Kennedy and Johnson, and the more than 400 African American officials elected to public office brought important changes in American society that finally affected the language issue. The Voting Rights Act of 1965, which ensured that African Americans in certain southern states would be able to participate through the ballot, also made it possible for Spanish-speaking Puerto Ricans living in New York State to vote.

Language legislation was given important support by President Johnson's "War on Poverty" in the mid-1960s. The President announced that the nation must embark on massive efforts to raise income levels and reduce unemployment. Public opinion supported all these efforts to rid the country of misery and the remnants of racial discrimination and looked to the public schools as the major instrument of social change. Prior to 1960, America's public schools were almost exclusively supported by states, counties, and towns; but by the 1960s, Americans supported the idea that schools could play an increased role in social change. In response, Congress passed the Elementary and Secondary Education Act of 1965. New opportunities opened for all Americans as segregation and discrimination declined and as organized help for the poor began in a much more extensive way than ever before.

The tense political environment of the civil rights era mounted an enormous pressure on the government to provide a bilingual education program. Responding to these pressures, Senator Ralph Yarborough of Texas set up a special Subcommittee on Bilingual Education in 1966. This subcommittee held hearings in Texas, California, and New York. These states had and continue to have a high density of language-minority groups and children who stand to gain from a bilingual education program. The hearings were highly politicized and the process produced many advocates of bilingual education on the Hill. By 1967, about 43 separate bills on bilingual education were introduced in the House of Representatives (Stoller 1976, Hakuta

1986). Consequently, a lengthy debate ensued in the House as part of the transformational process or the "dance of legislation." After the debate, the bills were narrowed down to a manageable document and on May 24, 1967, the House voted for the legislation. The same process was replicated in the Senate and the bill became law in January 1968.

In this very favorable context, educators, Mexican Americans, and other community leaders urged the Congress and President to assist those Americans who, because of their inability to use English well, could not participate fully in American society. The relative poverty of Spanish speakers linked the call to action with other social programs. The new separatist message of the "black power" movement motivated some intellectuals and political leaders to speak and write about a need to recognize America as a culturally plural society. This led senators and House members from California and Texas, two powerful states with significant Spanish-speaking populations, to sponsor and promote the legislation (Judd 1977:62).

Legislative Actions Leading to the Bilingual Education Act of 1968

As mentioned in previous chapters, many developments of the civil rights era witnessed a dramatic expansion of the federal government's role in the field of education. Historically, education had remained within the jurisdiction of state and local governments. The Morill Act of 1862 marked the beginning of federal involvement in national educational affairs, but this role did not progress significantly until the mid-1960s. Federal fundings were limited to monies rather than general subsidies. The 1965 ESEA was the catalyst for this new federal role in education. The Act was broad in its application and became the first general aid to education to be passed by Congress. The Act provided funds to school districts based on the number of low-income children in an area. The bulk of the money from federal aid was concentrated in the inner cities and rural areas where most poor children resided. These funds were also made available to private schools through such programs as shared-time services, loans of federally financed textbooks, etc.

Also in 1965, Congress passed the Higher Education Act. This law further broadened the federal government's role in education and, for the first time in American history, Congress authorized scholarships for undergraduate students based on financial need. The same Act authorized federal interest subsidies on private loans for middle income students. The

Teacher Corps program was also a by-product of the 1965 Higher Education Act. The dramatic federal role in education later culminated in the passage of the 1968 Bilingual Education Act, which was an amended version of Title VII of the ESEA (US Congress 1969:663–664).

The 1968 Bilingual Education Act provided aid to school districts with large numbers of children whose native languages were other than English (details of this legislation are provided in chapter five). As noted in chapter one, these children are also referred to as language minority, limited English proficient (LEP) or non-English proficient (NEP) students. At the initiation of Congress, particularly the delegates from Texas and California, in response to pressures from language-minority groups and civil rights activists, a program to improve the education of children from non-English–speaking families was authorized in 1967. About three million children of school age were expected to benefit from special programs funded under this bilingual education legislation. Although $40 million was authorized for aid to school districts and teacher training in fiscal 1969, the actual appropriation was only $7.5 million. This represented the first such appropriation under the bilingual education program. By contrast, the states had submitted some requests for over $40 million, proposing projects in 17 different languages. The emphasis, however, was on teaching children of Mexican and Puerto Rican backgrounds. The significance of ESEA was that it broke the impasse that had for long stymied legislators' efforts to provide federal aid to elementary and secondary schools in the United States. ESEA resulted in H.R. 2362–PL89–10, which authorized the first general school aid in the nation's history. The success of the bill was largely due to the compromised wording that skillfully avoided the past problems of public-private school funding debates (US Congress 1969:7–13).

Several new programs were established in the 1967 law which authorized a bilingual education project for children from a non-English–speaking background. Additional fellowships were awarded to teachers of these children and pilot projects were established to develop effective programs, prevent school dropouts, and provide technical assistance to rural schools that wished to apply for federal aid. It is important to note that although the mood of Congress was conservative in the 1960s (see details in chapter two), and its primary concerns were about crime, inflation, and riots on campuses around the country, it had a very productive legislative session (refer to chapter five for more on this). Many landmark bills were passed, particularly in the civil rights area. Congress, of course, was responding to pressures from the civil rights movement, the economic conditions of the nation, and various international forces. The importance of education was quite obvious to all Americans since illiteracy was frequently associated with poverty, unequal opportunity, low self-esteem, and crime. A litany of laws relating to education including, but not limited to, the National Defense Education Act, the Higher Education Act, the Economic Opportunity Act, the Adult Education Act, the Elementary and Secondary Education Act, and, of course, the Bilingual Education Act of 1968 were passed. The Bilingual Education Act, thus, was a by-product of the civil rights movement and the new awareness and prominence of education on the American policy agenda (US Congress 1969:726).

The "Legislative Dance" of the 1968 Bilingual Education Act

The "legislative dance" of the 1968 Bilingual Education Act was ushered in by a very important report: the *1960 Census Report*. This report was particularly significant because it provided the "beat" for the "dance." The report highlighted the new demographic trend of the growth of the Spanish-speaking population in the southwest and other parts of the country. The 1960 figures compared to those of 1950 revealed that the Hispanic populations in the five southwestern states of California, Arizona, Colorado, Texas, and New Mexico had increased by more than 50 percent. In Texas, the Hispanic population was 1,417,810, accounting for approximately 15 percent of the total population of 9.5 million people. California had the highest growth of the Hispanic population to the tune of an 87.6 percent increase over the 1950 figures (Leibowitz 1980:9, *1960 Census Report*). It was, therefore, not a coincidence that Senators Yarborough, Hawkins, Gonzales, and others who sponsored and/or supported the bill came from those states with large numbers of LEP and NEP children. In New York City, there were over 600,000 Puerto Ricans whose native tongue was Spanish; by 1966, they represented nearly 21 percent of the public school population (US Congress 1967).

Based on this report, Congress started debating the legislative details of the bills introduced. At this juncture, the federal government and the individual states were simultaneously responding to this increased constituency. This led to the establishment of the Interagency Committee on Mexican American Affairs (ICMAA) in 1965 by the federal government. (This committee later became the Cabinet Committee on Opportunity for the Spanish-Speaking [CCOSS] under President Nixon.) In 1967, a Mexican Affairs unit began to operate within the United States Office of Education. The response to this new and increased bloc of Americans continued. A few years later, the Equal Employment Opportunity Commission (EEOC) published its first study of Mexican Americans. The United States Commission on Civil Rights (USCCR) held its first hearing on Mexican Americans and published its report, *Mexican Americans and the Administration of Justice in the Southwest*, based on the hearing (Leibowitz 1980:11). These series of activities impacted heavily on the legislative process and further supported the system's framework with its emphasis on the interaction between the system's components. In this case, the political process was responding to external factors in the discourse of bilingual education legislation, and the debate on the floor was based on what was perceived to be a problem in the entire political system.

The level of education and the attrition rate of Spanish-speaking children were major concerns to Spanish-speaking parents, community leaders, and their advocates (see chapter two for details). The *1960 Census Report* on the educational level of Hispanic students in the five southwestern states indicated that Mexican American children had completed an average of 8.12 years of schooling, four years less than their Anglo American mates. The problems of Spanish speakers were so severe that Senator Yarborough limited his bill to Spanish-speaking children and made strong arguments for its justification in Senate debates. He made the following statement:

> We have limited this bill to the Spanish language because there are so many more of them than any other group. If you spread this idea to every language, it will fragment and destroy the bill. There is also a basic difference between the Spanish-speaking and other non-English-speaking groups. If you take the Italians, Polish, French, Germans, Norwegians, or other non-English-speaking groups, they made a definite decision to live their old life and culture and come here to a new country and set up a new way of life in accordance with ours, we assumed that they were giving up their language too.... That wasn't true in the Southwest. We went in and took the people over, took over the land and culture. They had our culture superimposed on them. They did not consent to abandon their homeland to come here and learn anew. They are not only the far more numerous group, but we recognize the fact that they are entitled to a special consideration (US Congress 1967:37).

Because of the large number of Spanish-speaking children, their plight became the dominant force behind the bilingual education debate in Congress. However, language problems were ubiquitous in many parts of the United States among Native American, Polish, French, Germans, Italians, and other non-English-speaking American communities. This problem was particularly severe among Native American children. The 1950 Indian Policy focused on terminating federal recognition of the Native American tribes, eliminating services, and relocating the Native Americans into cities (Leibowitz 1980:10). Based on these facts, the limitations of Senator Yarborough's bill to Spanish-speaking children was sharply attacked by other members of Congress, bureaucrats, and educators. Schmuel Lapin, General Secretary of the YIVO Institute of Jewish Research at the time, made the following statement:

> It is most doubtful whether the goals of these measures can be attained if its (sic) provisions are limited to one language and one culture alone. Unless all Americans regardless of their national origin are made to feel that preservation of various languages and cultures brought here by immigrants is important to the United States, there is little reason to believe that such a program restricted to Spanish alone can be successful (US Congress 1967:602).

As pointed out earlier, similar bills were introduced in the House of Representatives by Congressmen Augustus Hawkins and Edward Roybal of California and Jerome Scheuer of New York (US Congress 1967). The former expanded the Senate bill to include French-speaking, and the latter provided bilingual programs for all children whose native tongue was not English.

It was obvious from the debates in both Houses of Congress that the Hispanic population outnumbered the rest of the LEP and NEP children, and that the former group was to gain the most from a bilingual education program. However, that was not a justification for the exclusion of other groups with the same basic problems. In the Congressional Record of the 1967 Senate Hearings on Bilingual Education Programs, the following statement can be found:

> The primary beneficiary of any nationwide bilingual education program would undoubtedly be the Spanish-speaking children. But, there are also other groups of children needing special programs whose home language is not Spanish. There are French-speaking children in Louisiana and near the Canadian border, children of oriental, and American Indians in significant numbers in various areas. We expect that the number of children from other linguistic groups will increase in the next

few years as a result of last year's Liberalization of Immigration Act (US Congress 1967:33-34).

The legislative process continued in both Houses of Congress and extended to the other language-minority groups. Specific actions were taken to address the problems of Native American children. The roots for these actions can be traced back to the Eisenhower and Kennedy presidencies. During the latter part of the Eisenhower Administration, the "Indian Policy of Termination" was watered down. When President Kennedy took office, he declared his intent to reverse the policy. A task force was appointed to examine the status of Native American affairs. This task force looked into bilingualism in Native American education and recommended that the Bureau of Indian Affairs make special efforts to keep up with language training, instruction, and in-service training programs. Additional funds were made available to the Bureau and special innovation centers were set up to develop new educational methodologies for Native Americans. Obviously, the Native American educational policy had become so flawed that something had to be done. In the words of Leibowitz,

> In the 1800s the Cherokees had an educational system which produced a population of 90% literate in its native language and used bilingual materials to such an extent that Oklahoma Cherokees had a higher English literacy level than the white population of either Texas or Arkansas; in 1969 40% of adult Cherokees were functionally illiterate (1980:11; for more, see also US Congress 1969).

In response to these developments, President Johnson delivered a message on Native American affairs in Congress in which he emphasized the need for the improvement of education for Native Americans, control of Native American schools by Native American school boards, and language and cultural reinforcement. In the words of the President, "These schools will have the finest teachers, familiar with Indian history, culture, language—feature an enriched curriculum...a sound program to teach English as a second language" (US Congress HR Document 272).

It is also important to note that besides the preceding political developments, there were other international factors that brought about new interests in the introduction of foreign language programs in elementary and secondary schools. The federal government provided funds in the form of grants under the National Defense Education Act (NDEA) passed in 1958 in response to the Russian launching of the Sputnik. Several provisions of this

Act called for the retention and expansion of the nation's foreign language resources. Title VI and XI of the NDEA were frequently cited as justification for a strong national language policy during the 1967 hearings on the Bilingual Education Act.

This chapter on the legislative system focuses on the congressional processes that transformed the inputs into outputs. In other words, attention is directed at the third major research question of this study: What shaped the role played by the legislative branch in transforming inputs into outputs? David Easton's "authoritative allocation of values for society" and what was earlier referred to as the "dance of legislation" are at the core of this chapter. The preceding analysis is akin to Helen Ingram and Dean Mann's (1980:20) observation about public policy: legislation is sometimes targeted toward making people feel better instead of causing events to occur.

Chapter 5

OUTPUTS

This chapter examines the American political system's responses to demands (actual and anticipated) for the passage of the 1968 Bilingual Education Act and its aftermath. In addition, the part the outputs played in the coping processes are also looked at. This is important because outputs emanate from the political system in the forms of decisions (or nondecisions) and policy outcomes. These feed back into the environment by satisfying the demands of some members of the system, thereby generating support for the system. There may be negative consequences too, resulting in new demands in the system.

The Bilingual Education Act of 1968

The Bilingual Education Act of 1968 (see Appendix A) or Title VII of the Elementary and Secondary Education Act of 1965, as amended, provided supplemental funding for school districts interested in establishing programs to meet the "special educational needs of large numbers of children of limited English speaking (LEP) ability in the United States" (US Congress 1975:171). The children served under Title VII also had to be from low-income families (US Congress 1970:171). Funding was provided for planning, developing, and operating bilingual education programs; preservice training; early childhood and adult education; student retention programs; vocational training programs; and developing courses dealing with the history and culture of the language-minority group being served (US Congress 1970:171). Between 1969 and 1973, $117.9 million was expended under Title VII as follows: in 1967, $6.7 million; in 1970, $19 million; in 1971, $25.5 million;

in 1972, $33.5 million; in 1973, $33.2 million (USCCR 1975:171). Most of
this money went for support of bilingual programs in elementary schools. Of
this amount, 12 percent was spent for special bilingual education projects,
including bilingual children's television, curriculum centers, and a dissemination center. The special projects launched were as follows: Project BEST
(testing), New York City, New York, $1.6 million; Bilingual Children's
Television, Berkeley, California, $2.4 million; curriculum development
project, San Diego, California, $2 million; curriculum development project,
Miami, Florida, $2.7 million; dissemination center, Austin, Texas, $2.3
million; and school in Stockton, California, $2.3 million.

A major shortcoming of the 1968 Act was its failure to systematize means
of determining success in programs funded under the Act. Thus, after the first
five years, little was known about what comprised successful programs or what
progress had been made to overcome the obstacles faced by language-minority
children in school.

The first portion of an evaluation of Title VII programs was completed
in December 1973. That portion did not evaluate how well Title VII
programs improved students' educational performance. Instead, the emphasis
was on the extent to which Title VII projects adhered to guidelines and the
relationship between such adherence and project success. Determinations of
success were based on subjective ratings on a scale of one to five assigned to
different program components by evaluation team leaders. The second part
of this evaluation, which was still in progress at the time, was supposed to
address the effects of programs on standardized tests and other measures of
student progress (US Congress 1975:171).

Feedback

The Bilingual Education Act of 1974

The Bilingual Education Act of 1974 (see Appendix B) superseded the 1968
Act. It was more explicit in intent and design. Children need no longer be
low income, a criterion that had previously prevented Title VII from meeting
the needs of large numbers of language-minority children. For the first time,
the federal government provided a definition of what constitutes a bilingual
education program as follows:

> Instruction given in, and study of, English and to the extent necessary to allow a
> child to progress effectively through the educational system, the native language of

the children of instruction is given with appreciation for the cultural heritage of such children, and with respect to elementary school instruction, such instruction shall, to the extent necessary, be in all courses or subjects of study which will allow a child to progress effectively through the educational system (US Congress 1975:172).

The Act goes on to stipulate that in such courses as art, music, and physical education, LEP children should be in regular classes in the school. Support was provided for bilingual programs, supplemental community activities, training programs, fellowships, planning for programs, and technical assistance. Additional features included a requirement that the Commissioner of NACBE (set up under Title VII) report to Congress on the state of bilingual education in the nation. This report would provide information on the educational needs of children and others of limited English-speaking ability, Title VII activities, teacher and other bilingual personnel requirements, and the subsequent year's intended bilingual education activities and their cost (US Congress 1975:172–173).

Under the new legislation, a separate provision authorized an appropriation of $40.25 million over a five-year period under which State education agencies were eligible to receive training grants, along with local school districts and institutions of higher education. Most important, it called for research to be conducted by the National Institute of Education (NIE) of the Department of Health, Education and Welfare (HEW) for purposes of developing and disseminating instructional materials and equipment for bilingual education programs nationwide. In addition, the Secretary of Interior was charged with providing an annual assessment of the needs of Native American students for bilingual education and a review and evaluation of the use of bilingual education funds (US Congress 1975:173–174).

While the new bilingual legislation appeared to overcome many of the problems in the old Act, the nature of evaluation was still not clear and support for the overall program was limited. Although the Act received authorizations of $135 million, $140 million, $150 million, and $160 million for each of four years, Congress voted only $85 million for the first year's actual appropriation (US Congress 1975:174).

The Equal Educational Opportunity Act of 1974

Title II of the Education Amendments of 1974 or the Equal Educational Opportunity Act of 1974 did not have as its purpose an expansion of means for increasing equal educational opportunities. Instead, it imposed stringent congressional limitations on the use of transportation or "busing" as a means for overcoming discrimination based on race, color, sex, or national origin. Thus, it seriously hampered the abilities of federal courts and HEW to seek the most comprehensive remedy possible in cases of school segregation (US Congress 1975:175).

The Act declared congressional policy as follows: (1) that all children enrolled in public schools were entitled to equal education opportunity, regardless of race, color, sex, or national origin; and (2) that public school assignments should be based on the neighborhood in which children reside (US Congress 1975:176). Aside from raising formidable obstacles against the use of transportation to achieve desegregation, the Act provided a list of aspects that Congress defined as constituting a denial of equal educational opportunity. The major one is as follows: "the failure by an educational agency to take appropriate action to overcome language barriers that impede equal participation by its students in its instructional program" (US Congress 1975:176).

The Act provided for the initiation of civil action by individuals denied equal educational opportunity. Thus, it provided a direct statutory right of action to language-minority persons seeking to vindicate their rights to equal educational opportunity through the institution of effective language programs in the public schools.

Enforcement

The May 25 Memorandum

In this memorandum, HEW stipulated that school districts with more than five percent national-origin minority-group children have an obligation under Title VII to equal educational opportunity for language-minority students. Seventy-two districts, or four percent of all districts with five percent or more language-minority children, were reviewed by the agency's Office for Civil Rights (OCR) to determine their compliance with provisions of the memorandum (US Congress 1970:177).

Although school districts were required to provide some form of language program to meet the needs of language-minority children, the May 25 Memorandum did not specify what type of program this should be. Nevertheless, when a district did not provide an educational program for language-minority students, the agency strongly suggested that a curriculum be developed which did not penalize language-minority students for their language and culture. For example, following its on-site review of the El Paso Independent School District, HEW made the following recommendation concerning the type of plan which must be developed to overcome discrimination against language-minority students:

> Such a plan will include, among other things, an affirmative policy of recruiting and employing teachers who are bilingual and sensitive to these cultural differences; and a staff development program designed to assist teachers and administrators in redefining their role in a bilingual/bicultural district and in the development of a curriculum that does not penalize students who come to school with principal language skills in Spanish (US Congress 1975:177).

The school district submitted a plan which included a general outline of its intention to have an adequate representation of minority and bilingual teachers by 1977 (US Congress 1975:177). In addition, the school district proposed that a program be instituted in which both Spanish-speaking and English-speaking children would develop skills in the native language, while receiving intensive second language instruction. The plan was accepted by HEW (US Congress 1975:177).

Another school district, the Socorro Independent School District in Texas, was similarly required to submit a plan to provide language-minority students with an adequate educational program. The district indicated it would "attempt to develop a bilingual bicultural curriculum," hire bilingual aides, and introduce a language arts program using both Spanish and English for grades kindergarten through six (US Congress 1975:177).

HEW has the authority to withdraw federal financial assistance in cases where school districts are found in noncompliance and are unwilling to submit satisfactory plans to correct discrimination. There has been only one enforcement proceeding under the May 25 Memorandum. On the basis of noncompliance, HEW charged the Uvalde Independent School District with unlawful segregation of Mexican American students in elementary schools, discriminatory ability grouping, and failure to provide bilingual/bicultural education (US Congress 1975:178). The administrative law judge found that schools were illegally segregated, but declared the school district to be in compliance in the other three areas (US Congress 1975:178).

Following *Lau v Nichols* (see Appendix C for details), however, the Reviewing Authority reversed the administrative law judge on two of those three issues. The failure to provide bilingual/bicultural education and the nature of the district's practices of grouping students based on their abilities did deny the language-minority students equal educational opportunity, according to the Reviewing Authority (US Congress 1975:178). In requiring that bilingual/bicultural education be undertaken in order to provide equal educational opportunity for language-minority students, the Reviewing Authority took the strongest official federal position thus far on what constitutes compliance with the May 25 Memorandum (US Congress 1975; see also Appendix C).

The case of *Lau v Nichols* was a class suit which charged the San Francisco Unified School District with failure to provide all non-English–speaking students with special instruction to equalize their educational opportunity. The plaintiffs contended that their rights had been abridged under the United States Constitution, the California Constitution Title VI of the Civil Rights Act of 1964, and provisions of the California Education Code. They also cited the case of *Brown v Board of Education* (US Congress 1975:179; see Appendix D for details).

After being denied relief at lower court levels, the case was appealed to the Supreme Court. In January 1974, the Court ruled that there had been a denial of equal educational opportunity under Title VI of the Civil Rights Act of 1964 (US Congress 1970:179). The Court chose not to rule on whether there had been a violation of Constitutional rights. The case was remanded to the United States District Court for the fashioning of an appropriate remedy for the discrimination.

The school district has been working with a citizens' task force to develop the remedy. The *Lau* remedy promises to set the example for other districts contemplating their responsibilities to provide equal educational opportunity for language-minority students. HEW has also been involved in formulation of the remedy, since its interest is that the remedy be consistent with standards adopted by HEW in enforcement of the May 25 Memorandum.

Responses from State and Local Governments

State and local governments responded positively to the 1974, *Lau* decision by generally improving their programs and strengthening legal protection for linguistic-minority students. After the *Lau* decision, the number of states that launched bilingual education legislation more than doubled; others repealed statutes declaring English the sole language of instruction. State programs were designed after the Bilingual Education Act, as amended in 1974 and the *Lau* guidelines. Furthermore, states' funding for bilingual education increased (Moran 1988:1283).

Although some states followed the federal government's lead, they often designed legislation that reflected their unique needs. California's Chacon-Moscone Bilingual-Bicultural Education Act, for example, recognized the absence of qualified personnel and placed special emphasis on training bilingual educators and administrators. Proponents of the Act highlighted economic concerns to garner support for the program and carefully took into account implementation problems that state and local administrators would encounter (Moran 1988:1282–1283).

By the 1970s, Congress had become wary of prescribing particular educational techniques in light of the growing disparity of expert opinions regarding the value of native-language instruction. In addition, Congress was becoming quite concerned about the segregative effects of certain bilingual education programs. This led state and local policymakers to cease the opportunity to recover their decision-making prerogatives in the area of education. Meanwhile, judicial decisions raised questions about the validity of an effects test for discrimination against linguistic-minority groups. The Office for Civil Rights (OCR) finally withdrew the *Lau* guidelines in the face of a procedural assault. Also, the Department of Education failed to offer alternative rules because of widespread disaffection with bilingual programs, pedagogical uncertainties about their effectiveness, and an alliance between state and local educators and English-only advocates who sought to end federal funding for bilingual-bicultural programs (Moran 1988:1282).

Consequently, Congress reconsidered the Bilingual Education Act in 1977. The most influential material presented during the hearing was the study of bilingual education programs conducted by the American Institute for Research (AIR). The study was commissioned by the Office of Planning, Budget, and Evaluation (OPBE) in response to a congressional directive that the Office of Education assess the status of federally funded bilingual education projects. The study's major focus was on whether the programs were helping the targeted students acquire English while progressing in other school subjects through use of their native language. The AIR investigators were able to conduct a comprehensive study because of federal financial support. Approximately 286 bilingual education classrooms in 38 Spanish/English projects in operation for at least four years as of 1975 were examined. Due to its "official status," the study generated a great deal of influence and media attention (Moran 1988:1285; AIR 1977–1978).

A great deal of controversy resulted because of the findings of the AIR study. First, students in bilingual education programs received slightly lower scores than comparable students in regular programs on English tests. Second, students in bilingual education programs performed somewhat better than comparable students in regular programs on mathematics tests. Third, no significant difference existed in the attitudes toward school children in bilingual education programs and regular programs. Fourth, the ability of students in bilingual education programs to read Spanish improved greatly. Fifth, less than one-third of the students in bilingual education programs had limited-English proficiency, despite the fact that three-quarters of them were Hispanic. Finally, over 85 percent of the bilingual education projects retained students in bilingual classrooms after they were sufficiently proficient in English to function in regular classroom settings (Moran 1988:1285; AIR 1977–1978).

As is to be expected, the AIR study encountered strong criticism. The Director of OBE, John Molina, for example, attacked the utility of the evaluation process itself:

> You actually can't evaluate a bilingual education program. It is philosophy and management. You can evaluate courses. For example, evaluation should be limited to reading, mathematics, science and social science. I think we need a tremendous amount of research in order to determine what are the best methods and if children learn in languages other than English (Moran 1988:1285–1286; US Congress 1977:69).

In addition to attacking the methodological shortcomings of the AIR study, a number of witnesses pointed out that bilingual education programs had been subjected to a double standard. They noted that no other educational program had so harshly been evaluated, criticized, and scrutinized like the bilingual education program (Moran 1988:1286; US Congress 1977:69).

When the Senate subcommittee on education held hearings a few months later, members downplayed the AIR controversy. It solicited testimony from only a selected group of supporters of the native-language instruction strategy. Many of the members on the panel concluded that research done by OPBE, including the AIR study, was inadequate mainly because the organizations lacked bilingual education experts. As such, a number of the witnesses urged Congress to accord a larger research role to OBE. They also called for greater supervision of programs by OBE to make sure that poor outcomes did not result from ineffective implementation (Moran 1988:1286; US Congress 1977:820-822).

However, some congressmen had concerns about program objectives because many project directors and staff retained children in bilingual class-rooms after they had achieved English-language proficiency. For these congressmen, such a practice exhibited a perpetuation of a pluralist, rather than an assimilationist, approach (Moran 1988:1287; US Congress 1977:156-158). In addition, they feared that retaining children in bilingual education classes could turn experimental research into service programs. Such an outcome would undermine the federal government's original intent to play only a temporary role in funding bilingual education programs (Moran 1988:1287; US Congress 1977:63-67).

Using more explicit legislation, Congress sought to limit bilingual educators' discretion over long-term programs that were inconsistent with the objectives of the Bilingual Education Act. House members insisted that the Act clarify the objectives of enabling targeted students to participate in regular classrooms. The House and Senate mandated that the federal government's role be limited to short-term grants that would assist state and local governments in delivering bilingual education services. Significantly, the House called for the minimization of segregation of linguistic-minority students by placing English-speaking students in bilingual classrooms (Moran 1988:1289; US Congress 1977:85-87).

The amended Act took into account the concerns raised. To begin with, the Act's major objective was clarified as follows: "to the extent necessary to allow a child to achieve competence in the English language" (Moran 1988:1289; US Congress 1982). It is very clear from this statement that Congress intended the ultimate goal of bilingual education programs to be English-acquisition instruction.

As Moran succinctly concludes, the AIR study controversy highlighted the dilemmas inherent in the Bilingual Education Act's odd marriage of civil rights rhetoric to the federal educational bureaucracy. The 1978 amendments to the Act reinstated the research and development orientation that was more congruent with the general role of the federal education bureaucracy. The civil rights feature that survived this retrenchment under the Act was the one most firmly established: the principle of desegregation (1988:1291. With the 1978 amendments firmly in place, it was not until 1981 that major concerns began to emerge over the federal government's role in bilingual-bicultural education.

The Office of Planning, Budget and Evaluation (OPBE) 1981 Report

In October 1981, OPBE released a report it commissioned Beatrice Birman and Alan Ginsburg (1981, 1983) to prepare. The report acknowledged that linguistic-minority students needed some form of educational assistance, but questioned the type of assistance that was being offered and the rationale for the federal government's role. Birman and Ginsburg posited that the educational hardships of linguistic-minority students emanated from poverty as well as language. Thus, according to these authors, bilingual education programs comprised a partial solution, particularly in the cases of students from economically deprived homes who lacked proficiency in both English and their native language (see also Moran 1988:1299). This argument clearly undermined the civil rights basis for providing bilingual-bicultural and transitional bilingual education programs. As to be expected, the Birman-Ginsburg report faced scathing criticism just as the AIR study before it.

The authors also found that the federal government's overwhelming dependence on transitional bilingual education (TBE) programs was unwarranted because little evidence existed to support their superiority over alternative strategies. The authors thus recommended that the federal government consider promising approaches to TBE programs, especially structured emersion strategies. Furthermore, they called for greater discretion by state and local educators in designing and implementing bilingual education programs (Birman and Ginsburg 1981:515–516). By the following year (1982), the Senate was so concerned about the findings of the report that it called for a hearing on the Bilingual Education Act.

The 1982 Senate Hearings on the Bilingual Education Act

When Congress held hearings on the Bilingual Education Act in 1982, its expressed intention was to amend the Act. It received testimony from federal administrators responsible for overseeing the implementation of the Act, state representatives and local educators responsible for delivering services, and

Hispanic leaders. Two major issues were tackled: (1) whether bilingual education programs were promoting separatism; and (2) how to allocate the responsibility of designing and implementing the programs to local, state, and federal governments. Furthermore, Congress considered decreasing funds for the programs (US Congress 1982).

During the hearings, a group of English-only reformers—commonly known as US English (USE), led by Senator S. I. Hayakawa, raised concerns about the divisive nature of bilingual education programs. This group sought to support programs that do not promote native-language instruction at the expense of English. It also predicted that within the next 10 to 20 years, states in which the majority of the residents speak languages other than English will choose those tongues as their official languages. The group's leading spokesperson, Senator Hayakawa, went on to state,

> Learning English has been the primary task of every immigrant group for two centuries. Participation in the common language has rapidly made the political and economic benefits of American society available to every new group as they came in, and those who have mastered English have overcome the major hurdles to participation in our democracy (Moran 1988:20).

In supporting USE's position, Senator Walter D. Huddleston added that Congress should make sure that "we are indeed helping nonnative-born students achieve proficiency in our own common language and are helping to rapidly assimilate them into our society" (Moran 1988:41). For Huddleston, Congress's initial intent was to support programs that promptly mainstreamed students who mastered English, not programs which sought to achieve linguistic pluralism. He went on to suggest that any provision for foreign language training should be submitted in a separate legislation (US Congress 1982:44–45).

Supporters of bilingual education programs were quick to counter the views of their opponents. For the former group, the latter's arguments were thinly veiled in racism that require LEP and NEP students to treat their own language and culture as inferior to English. Echoing the sentiment of supporters of bilingual education programs, Arnoldo S. Tores, National Executive Director of the League of United Latin American Citizens (LULAC), linked the attacks on bilingual education to the increase in anti-immigrant feelings. Dismissing the claim that bilingual education programs promoted separatism, Tores stated the following:

> Our purpose in supporting these programs is precisely that of helping students to be better contributors to mainstream American society. Those who insist on regulating minority-language students to an inferior status by placing them in situations where they are doomed to lag behind or fail are those who are actually promoting a continued separation due to lack of communication and achievement (Moran 1988:1249; US Congress 1982:111).

Another major speaker during the 1982 Senate hearings on bilingual education programs was then Secretary of Education Terrel H. Bell. His main focus was on the allocation of responsibility for bilingual education programs among federal, state, and local governments. For Bell, the federal government was to be the catalyst for bilingual education programs by providing startup funds; state and local governments were to take up the programs once they became operational (US Congress 1982:3–5).

Those who feared that state and local officials were indifferent, and in some cases hostile, to LEP and NEP students' needs favored retention of federal civil rights protection (Moran 1988:1249). As Delia Pompa, Executive Director of Bilingual Education for the Houston Independent School District, argued, proposed cutbacks in federal funding would be harmful in districts that lack the necessary resources to conduct research on costly programs for LEP and NEP students. Instead, Pompa added, school administrators in those districts will opt for the least expensive strategies that relied heavily on English (US Congress 1982:171–172). With this debate in mind, the House took up the Bilingual Education Improvement Act the following year (1983).

The 1983 Bilingual Education Improvement Act

The 1983 Bilingual Education Improvement Act was introduced in the House of Representatives at the same time that a similar bill was being considered in the Senate. According to Secretary Bell, the 1983 Act's major goals were (1) to give school districts greater latitude in choosing among available approaches to serve the needs of LEP and NEP children; (2) to limit federal grants to five-year periods while supporting school districts' capacity to continue programs after grants were terminated; (3) to strengthen the role of state educational agencies in making and implementing bilingual education policies; (4) to define the target population of LEP and NEP students more stringently in order to effectively allocate federal funds; and (5) to authorize adult bilingual education programs under the Bilingual Education Act, instead of the Vocational Education Act (Moran 1988:1305; US Congress 1983:22–23).

Soliciting testimony from federal, state, and local officials responsible for administering bilingual education programs, two representatives from teachers' organizations and one Hispanic businessman, the House subcommittee on education focused on encouraging program flexibility and decreasing federal funding. A number of school administrators and House members (especially Representative Ron Packard of California; Albert Shanker, President of the American Federation of Teachers; Diane Ravitch, Adjunct Associate Professor, Teachers College, Columbia University; Jolly Ann Davidson, President-Elect, National Association of State Boards of Education; and Esther Eisenhower, Director, English-as-a-Second-Language Program, Fairfax County, Virginia Public Schools) called for approval of efforts to expand the scope of programs supported under the Act. Bilingual educators (particularly Awilda Orta, Director, Bilingual Education Programs, New York City; Linda Tarr-Whelan, Director of Government Relations, National Education Association; James E. Alatis, President, Joint National Committee for Languages; Sau-Lim Tsang, Executive Director, ARC Associates, Inc., Oakland, California) countered with the argument that in its push for greater flexibility the federal government would leave schools districts with no meaningful guidelines to implement the programs (Moran 1988:1248–1249; US Congress 1983:31–151).

Despite the Reagan Administration's strong support, the 1983 Bilingual Education Improvement Act was defeated in the House. Nonetheless, supporters of bilingual education programs did not give up, as evidenced the following year (1984).

The 1984 Reauthorization of the Bilingual Education Act

Energized by their efforts in 1983 and strong support from the Reagan Administration, proponents of TBE and bilingual-bicultural education programs introduced a relatively modest bill. Guided by Carl Perkins, Chair of the House Education and Labor Committee, the Act sought simply to reauthorize the Bilingual Education Act for another four years. Working with the National Association for Bilingual Education (NABE) and the National Council of La Raza (NCLR), Representatives Dale Kildee of Michigan and

Baltasar Corrada of Puerto Rico drafted an alternative bill that sought not only to strengthen the federal role in bilingual education programs, but also to strengthen the reliance on native-language instruction in educating LEP and NEP students (Moran 1988:1249).

However, following the debate over local and federal commitment to LEP students and withdrawal of the *Lau* provisions, the 1984 Bilingual Education Reauthorization Act provided greater flexibility for state and local school districts in bilingual education matters. It set a new precedence by allowing up to four percent of overall funds (or up to 10 percent if more than $140 million was appropriated in a single fiscal year) to go to special alternative instructional programs, which did not require that native language be used. Nonetheless, 75 percent of the funds for instructional programs were still allocated to TBE programs (Crawford 1984:19–50).

The 1984 amendments awarded grants for several types of special programs for LEP students. These programs included

1. transitional bilingual education programs, in which structured English language instruction is combined with a native language component and up to 40 percent of the class may be non-LEP students;

2. developmental bilingual education programs, in which full-time instruction is given in both English and a second language with the goal of achieving competence in both English and a second language;

3. special alternative instructional programs in which the native language need not be used, but English language instruction and special instructional services are given to facilitate achievement of English competency. (Depending on their needs, school districts were eligible to apply for these grants to promote the programs.) (NACBE 1979:5–6; US Congress 1984).

Furthermore, the amendments stipulated that parents or guardians take a major role in the education of their LEP children. Schools were charged with the responsibility of explaining to parents why their children were selected for the program and to inform them about alternative programs. The parents and guardians were also given the right to accept or reject enrollment of their children in bilingual education programs. The amendments also offered grants for academic excellence programs and family English literacy programs (NACBE 1979:6). The 1984 Act served its four-year course until 1988 when the most recent bilingual education legislation was enacted.

The 1988 Bilingual Education Act

The House Committee on Education and Labor, in conjunction with the Hispanic caucus, recognizing that the Bilingual Education Act would have to be reauthorized in 1988, held a hearing on bilingual education in early 1987. As Committee Chairman Augustus F. Hawkins suggested, the hearing would "put the [Reagan] Administration...on notice that our country cannot be competitive without a system of education which assures that all of our nation's children receive an equal educational opportunity" (Moran 1988:1249).

In response to the Office of Planning, Budget, and Evaluation's (OPBE) negative findings on TBE and bilingual-bicultural education programs, the House Committee requested a study on the research validity of the OPBE report to be conducted by the General Accounting Office (GAO). The GAO sent questionnaires to 10 educational experts. The results generated from the survey suggested that the OPBE consistently understated the benefits of bilingual education programs and overstated the potential benefits of alternative programs that utilize more English-language instruction. As to be expected, the GAO report, like the OPBE study it evaluated, generated considerable controversy. The Department of Education, for example, responded by questioning the validity of the survey methodology employed by the GAO, charging that the Agency's study had been politically motivated to embarrass the Reagan Administration (Moran 1988:1311–1312).

Despite the results of the GAO study, greater discretion was accorded state and local educators in their choice of instructional methods when the Act was reauthorized in 1988. To ensure state and local educators' hegemony in bilingual education, the Act specified that

> A state education agency is eligible for grants of at least $75,000, not to exceed 5 percent of the total funds awarded to that state under part A in the previous year. This reflects an increase from $50,000 in previous legislation (NACBE 1988:7).

In addition, a three-year limit was set on a student's participation in a TBE program or in special alternative instructional programs. Under special circumstances, however, a student could be allowed to continue in a program for up to two additional years (Moran 1988:1312).

The Act placed greater emphasis on training and retraining activities. In order to ensure that a pool of qualified personnel is available, Congress authorized that a minimum of 500 fellowships be awarded each year. Another new feature to the bill was that the first 12 months of a grant to a school district, rather than six months (as stipulated in previous legislation), could also be devoted to preservice activities. However, grants for instructional materials development were discontinued and the National Advisory and Coordinating Council on Bilingual Education (NACCBE) was eliminated (Moran 1988:1312).

The forgoing discussion shows that the Bilingual Education Act of 1968 has undergone many changes that reflect the needs of LEP and NEP students in the United States. It has been transformed from a tool for providing basic guidelines to one that provides concrete regulations and encourages greater local control of bilingual education curriculum. As it currently stands, the major emphasis of the Act is on assisting school districts in providing a variety of alternative strategies to enable LEP and NEP students to reach proficiency in English and to succeed in mainstream classes.

Although the education of LEP and NEP students has never been a smooth process, it has, nevertheless, evolved in an effort to better meet these students' needs. Changes in bilingual education simply reflect the evolution of public opinion as the United States struggles to accommodate its new immigrants.

An analysis of the outputs of the transformational process of the Bilingual Education Act of 1968 and its aftermath is the main point of this chapter. Attention is given to the fourth major research question of this book: What are the outputs of the transformational process and how can they be characterized? The Act has been reauthorized four times (1974, 1978, 1984, and 1988) since its original authorization in 1968. These subsequent authorizations emphasize the importance of the outputs and to some extent show the significance of the Act in dealing with the problems of language-minority children. They also stress the function and importance of the feedback mechanism in sustaining the use of the American political system.

Chapter 6

SUMMARY AND CONCLUSIONS

This book began by pointing out the need for a thorough examination of the role of the United States Congress in the passing of the 1968 Bilingual Education Act and its aftermath. This need hinged on the fact that most works on bilingualism in the United States concentrate on the linguistic and legal aspects of the issue, and very little attention has been paid to the legislative process (i.e., political) that led to the passage of the Act. Thus, existing works that have explored the conflict and controversy associated with bilingual education policies, programs, and practices miss defining, describing, or explaining the nature of this conflict and its impact on the evolution of bilingual education legislation with a sound theoretical basis.

In order to fill this gap in the literature of bilingual education in the United States, four major questions were investigated. These questions are as follows:

1. In what types of political, economic, social, and cultural environments did the debate on bilingual education emerge?

2. What are the positions of the competing factions that lobbied Congress on the issue of bilingual education, and how can they be characterized?

3. What shaped the roles played by the legislative branch in transforming inputs into outputs?

4. What are the outputs of the transformation processes, and how can they be characterized?

To explore these questions, pertinent data were collected from primary sources (face-to-face interviews and Congressional Records) and secondary sources (books, journal articles, newspaper articles, and magazine articles). The data collected were analyzed qualitatively; that is, a comprehensive description and explanation of the many data collected were done. To place the data analysis on sound theoretical footing, David Easton's "framework for political analysis" was employed. The findings derived from this analysis (see preceding chapters) make it possible to delineate a number of conclusions.

First, Easton's "framework for political analysis" appears quite adequate in analyzing the issue of bilingual education in the United States. In chapters three and four, it is shown that legislators responded to inputs in the form of demands and support from the Supreme Court, the executive branch, civil rights leaders, state and local administrators, education experts, and Hispanic parents and community leaders who believed in the legitimacy of these representatives. Chapter five shows how members of Congress formulated outputs (the 1968 Bilingual Education Act and subsequent amendments) and decisions about conflicting interests. In chapter two, it is revealed that Congress had to work within an altruistic, but volatile, environment and was forced to make policies in keeping with the American culture. Chapter five also reveals that policymakers did make use of feedback in order to maintain the survival of the American political system. This feedback took two forms: (1) proponents of bilingual education called for a program geared toward equalitarianism, and (2) opponents of the program asked for one that promotes the rapid assimilation of language-minority children into the Anglo-American cultural and linguistic norm. When opponents of the bilingual education program pressed their dissatisfaction, Congress moved to adjust the Bilingual Education Act accordingly.

Second, the 1964 election, which saw the Democratic Party dominate both the Senate and the House of Representatives, was crucial in getting Congress to pass the 1968 Bilingual Education Act. The significance of this election is that it smashed the conservative coalition made up of Republicans and Southern Democrats. This allowed President Lyndon Johnson to pass three major measures that had long been blocked by the coalition: civil rights, education, and Medicare.

Third, President Johnson's ideology and style were important in shaping the type of political environment conducive to the passage of the 1968 Bilingual Education Act. Johnson aspired to be a political leader with the talent at achieving reconciliation. He also believed that hospitable to democracy was the conviction that power and success must be employed to benefit others. Johnson's perceptions of the nature of power moved him more to the backstage than to the frontstage in the political drama. His manipulator-compromiser style carried a built-in cautionary device: nothing was ever final, and everything was susceptible to accommodation and adjustment.

Fourth, the timing of the Bilingual Education Act was opportune. The 1960s saw attempts by Americans to trace the satisfactions and disappointments attendant on great hopes. Many American citizens had become self-conscious of their identity and social function. Emerging definitions disregarded older ideas about the social order such as the idea that it was not mediation, privacy, and inner development that engaged those who located the citizen of thought, but action, public immersion, and power. Many felt that they should themselves supply to a democracy those public virtues not accounted for by mere electoral representation; all kinds of demands were being made, not the least of which is that decisionmakers should embody American morale impulses.

Fifth, the major thorn in the bilingual education program was and remains that of administration. Many of the goals for the program proclaimed by the national government have to be achieved through the administrative expertise of state and local governments, that legally are independent and some are even politically hostile. While the transformation of the federal system appears to have been accepted, the mechanisms that will make it work are yet to be perfected. Even if a national consensus about the value of bilingual education exists, there is no simple answer as to how to promote it. The issue, then, is whether the crises of race, poverty, and violence that press the need for bilingual education upon the country will tolerate a pause.

Sixth, although initially conceived as an enrichment program, the 1968 Bilingual Education Act had to be recast into a compensatory education program by the time it was signed into law because of the political climate of the time. The Act has also undergone many changes over the years: from offering only basic guidelines to providing more concrete regulations and encouraging greater local control of program curriculum. These changes reflect an evolution in public opinion as the United States accommodates new waves of immigrants. Even though controversy is the order of business in bilingual education, it has, nevertheless, evolved in attempts to better meet the needs of LEP and NEP students.

Seventh, education policy in the United States has become *increasingly* politicized because of the language issue. The language issue, in turn, arises because of (a) immigration, (b) attempts to integrate previously separated or even segregated populations, and (c) the emerging pride and assertiveness among ethnic groups. Schools therefore serve as the gateway to participation in the political and economic arena, and they help build a sense of national identity.

Finally, the bilingual education program will continue in the United States. Since the Congress and the courts have made clear that proficiency in English must be the goal, the great majority of projects will continue to be "transitional." That is, students will continue to learn to read and write in the language they already speak in order to facilitate a speedy transition to English. It also appears likely that the future of the program will depend upon establishing clear evaluative criteria and a record of success.

Appendices

Appendix A

Public Law 90–247–Jan. 2, 1968
Appropriations Authorized
Sec. 602. There is hereby authorized to be appropriated $150,000 to carry out the provisions of this title.

Title VII–Bilingual Education Programs
Findings of Congress
Sec. 701. The Congress hereby finds that one of the most acute educational problems in the United States is that which involves millions of children of limited English-speaking ability because they come from environments where the dominant language is other than English; that additional efforts should be made to supplement present attempts to find adequate and constructive solutions to this unique and perplexing educational situation; and that the urgent need is for comprehensive and cooperative action now on the local, state, and federal levels to develop forward-looking approaches to meet the serious learning difficulties faced by this substantial segment of the nation's school-age population.

Amendment to Elementary and Secondary Education Act of 1965
Sec. 702. The Elementary and Secondary Education Act of 1965 is amended by redesignating title VII as title VIII, by redesignating sections 701 through 707 and reference thereto as sections 801 through 807, respectively, and by inserting title VI the following new title (79 Stat. 55; 80 Stat. 1204, 20 USC 881, 886.):

"Title VII—Bilingual Education Programs
"Short Title
"Sec. 701. This title may be cited as the 'Bilingual Education Act'.

"Declaration of Policy
"Sec. 702. In recognition of the special educational needs of the large numbers of children of limited English-speaking ability in the United States, Congress hereby declares it to be the policy of the United States to provide financial assistance to local educational agencies to develop and carry out new and imaginative elementary and secondary school programs designed to meet these special educational needs. For the purposes of this title, 'children of limited English-speaking ability means children who come from environments where the dominant language is other than English.

"Authorization and Distribution of Funds
"Sec. 703. (a) For the purposes of making grants under this title, there is authorized to be appropriated the sum of $150,000,000 for the fiscal year ending June 30, 1968, $30,000,000 for the fiscal year ending June 30, 1969, and $40,000,000 for the fiscal year ending June 30, 1970.

"(b) In determining distribution of funds under this title, the Commissioner shall give highest priority to States and areas within States having the greatest need for programs pursuant to this title. Such priorities shall take into consideration the number of children of limited English-speaking ability between the ages of three and eighteen in each State.

"Sec. 704. Grants under this title may be used, in accordance with applications approved under section 705, for—

"(a) planning for and taking other steps leading to the development of programs designed to meet the special educational needs of children of limited English-speaking ability in schools having a high concentration of such children from families. (A) with incomes below $3,000 per year, or (B) receiving payments under a program of aid to families with dependent children under a State plan approved under title IV of the Social Security Act, including research projects, pilot projects designed to test the effectiveness of plans so developed, and the development and dissemination of special instructional materials for use in bilingual education programs (42 USC 401-428.); and

"(b) providing preservice training designed to prepare persons to participate in bilingual education programs as teachers, teacher-aides, or other ancillary education personnel such as counselors, and in-service training and development programs designed to enable such persons to continue to improve their qualifications while participating in such programs; and

"(c) the establishment, maintenance, and operation of programs, including acquisition of necessary teaching materials and equipment, designed to meet the special educational needs of children of limited English-speaking ability in schools having a high concentration of such children from families (A) with incomes below $3,000 per year; or (B) receiving payments under a program of aid to families with dependent children under a State plan approved under title IV of the Social Security Act, through activities such as—

"1. bilingual education programs;

"2. programs designed to impart to students a knowledge of the history and culture associated with their languages;

"3. efforts to establish closer cooperation between the school and the home;

"4. early childhood educational programs related to the purposes of this title and designed to improve the potential for profitable learning activities by children;

"5. adult education programs related to the purposes of this title, particularly for parents of children participating in bilingual programs;

"6. programs designed for dropouts or potential dropouts having need of bilingual programs;

"7. programs conducted by accredited trade, vocational, or technical schools; and

"8. other activities which meet the purposes of this title.

"Application for Grants and Conditions for Approval
"Sec. 705. (a) A grant under this title may be made to a local educational agency or agencies, or to an institution of higher education applying jointly with a local educational agency, upon application to the Commissioner at such time or times, in such manner and containing or accompanied by such information as the Commissioner deems necessary. Such application shall—

"1. provide that the activities and services for which assistance under this title is sought will be administered by or under the supervision of the applicant;

"2. set forth a program for carrying out the purpose set forth in section 704 and provide for such methods of administration as are necessary for the proper and efficient operation of the program;

"3. set forth a program of such size, scope, and design as will make a substantial step toward achieving the purpose of this title;

"4. set forth policies and procedures which assure that Federal funds made available under this title for any fiscal year will be so used as to supplement and, to the extent practicable, increase the level of funds (including funds made available under title I of this Act) that would, in the absence of such Federal funds, be made available by the applicant for the purposes described in section 704, and in no case supplant such funds (79 Stat. 27; 80 Stat. 1198, 20 USC 241a, note.);

"5. provide for such fiscal control and fund accounting procedures as may be necessary to assure proper disbursement of and accounting for Federal funds paid to the applicant under this title;

"6. provide for making an annual report and such other reports, in such form and containing such information, as the Commissioner may reasonably require to carry out his functions under this title and to determine the extent to which funds provided under this title have been effective in improving the educational opportunities of persons in the area served, and for keeping such records and for affording such access thereto as the Commissioner may find necessary to assure the correctness and verification of such reports;

"7. provide assurance that provision has been made for the participation in the project of those children of limited English-speaking ability who are not enrolled on a full-time basis; and

"8. provide that the applicant will utilize in programs assisted pursuant to this title the assistance of persons with expertise in the educational problems of children of limited English-speaking ability and make optimum use in such programs of the cultural and educational resources of the area to be served; and for the purposes of this paragraph, the term 'cultural and educational resources' includes State educational agencies, institutions of higher education, nonprofit private schools, public and nonprofit private agencies such as libraries, museums, musical and artistic organizations, educational radio and television, and other cultural and educational resources.

"(b) Applications for grants under title may be approved by the Commissioner only if—

"1. the application meets the requirements set forth in subsection (a);

"2. the program set forth in the application is consistent with criteria established by the Commissioner (where feasible, in cooperation with the State educational agency) for the purpose of achieving an equitable distribution of assistance under this title within each State, which criteria shall be developed by him on the basis of a consideration of (A) the geographic distribution of children of limited English-speaking ability, (B) the relative need of persons in different geographic areas within the State for the kinds of services and activities described in paragraph (c) of section 704, and (C) the relative ability of particular local educational agencies within the State to provide those services and activities;

"3. the Commissioner determines (A) that the program will utilize the best available talents and resources and will substantially increase the educational opportunities for children of limited English-speaking ability in the area to be served by the applicant, and (B) that, to the extent consistent with the number of children enrolled in nonprofit private schools in the area to be served whose educational needs are of the type which this program is intended to meet, provision has been made for participation of such children; and

"4. the State educational agency has been notified of the application and been given the opportunity to offer recommendations.

"(c) Amendments of applications shall, except as the Commissioner may otherwise provide by or pursuant to regulations, be subject to approval in the same manner as original applications.

"Payments

"Sec. 706. (a) The Commissioner shall pay to each applicant which has an application approved under this title an amount equal to the total sums expended by the applicant under the application for the purposes set forth therein.

"(b) Payments under this title may be made in installments and in advance or by way of reimbursement, with necessary adjustments on account of overpayments or underpayments.

"Advisory Committee

"Sec. 707. (a) The Commissioner shall establish in the Office of Education an Advisory Committee on the Education of Bilingual Children, consisting of nine members appointed, without regard to the civil service laws, by the Commissioner with the approval of the Secretary. The Commissioner shall appoint one such member as Chairman. At least four of the members of the Advisory Committee shall be educators experienced in dealing with the educational problems of children whose native tongue is language other than English.

"(b) The Advisory Committee shall advise the Commissioner in the preparation of general regulations and with respect to policy matters arising in the administration of this title, including the development of criteria for approval of applications thereunder. The Commissioner may appoint such special advisory and technical experts and consultants as may be useful and necessary in carrying out the functions of the Advisory Committee.

"(c) Members of the Advisory Committee shall, while serving on the business of the Advisory Committee, be entitled to receive compensation at rates fixed by the Secretary, but not exceeding $100 per day, including travel time; and while so serving away from their homes or regular place of business, they may be allowed travel expenses, including per diem in lieu of subsistence, as authorized by section 5703 of title 5 of the United States Code for persons in the Government service employed intermittently (Members Compensation travel expenses. 80 Stat, 499.).

"Labor Standards
"Sec. 708. All laborers and mechanics employed by contractors or sub-contractors on all minor remodeling projects assisted under this title shall be paid wages at rates not less than those prevailing on similar minor remodeling in the locality as determined by the Secretary of Labor in accordance with the Davis-Bacon Act, as amended (40 U.S.C. 276a–276a-5). The Secretary of Labor shall have, with respect to the labor standards specified in this section, the authority and functions set forth in Reorganization Plan Numbered 14 of 1950 and section 2 of the Act of June 13, 1934, as amended (40 U.S.C. 276c)." (49 Stat. 1011; 78 Stat. 238.; 64 Stat. 1267.; 63 Stat. 108.)

Conforming Amendments
Sec. 703. (a) That part of section 801 (as so redesignated by section 702 of this Act) of the Elementary and Secondary Education Act of 1965 which precedes clause (a) is amended by striking out "and VI" and inserting in lieu thereof "VI, and VII" (Ante, p. 816.).

(b) Clause (j) of such section 801 as amended by this Act is further amended by striking out "and VI" and inserting in lieu thereof "VI, and VII".

Amendments to Title V of the Higher Education Act of 1965
Sec. 704. (a) The third sentence of section 521 of the Education Professions Development Act (title V of the Higher Education Act of 1965) is amended (1) effective for the fiscal year ending June 30, 1968 only, by inserting after "a career of teaching in elementary or secondary schools" a new phrase as follows: "a career of teaching children of limited English-speaking ability", and (2) effective with respect to subsequent fiscal years, by inserting "and including teaching children of limited English-speaking ability" after "including teaching in pre-school and adult and vocational education programs." (79 Stat. 1258, 20 USC 1111; Ante, p. 93.)

(b) Effective for the fiscal year ending June 30, 1968, only, section 522(a) of such Act is amended by striking out "ten thousand fellowships for the fiscal year ending June 30, 1968" and inserting in lieu thereof "eleven thousand fellowships for the fiscal year ending June 30, 1968". (20 USC 1112.)

(c)(1) Section 528 of such Act is amended, effective with respect to fiscal years ending after June 30, 1967, by striking out "$275,000,000" and inserting in lieu thereof "$285,000,000"; striking out "$195,000,000" and inserting in lieu thereof "$205,000,000"; striking out "$240,000,000" and inserting in lieu thereof $250,000,000"; and striking out "July 1, 1968" and inserting in lieu thereof "July 1, 1970". (20 USC 1118.)

(2) The amendments made by this subsection shall, notwithstanding section 9(a) of Public Law 90-35, be effective with regard to fiscal years beginning after June 30, 1967. (Ante, p. 94.)

(d) Section 531(b) of such Act is amended by redesignating clauses (8) and (9) thereof as clauses (9) and (10), respectively, and by inserting immediately after clause (7) the following new clause (Ante, p. 92):

"(8) programs for projects to train or retrain persons engaging in special educational programs for children of limited English-speaking ability;".

Amendments to Title XI of the National Defense Education Act of 1958
Sec. 705. (a) Section 1101 of the National Defense Education Act of 1958 is amended by striking out "and for each of the two succeeding fiscal years" and inserting in lieu thereof "and for the succeeding fiscal year, and $51,000,000 for the fiscal year ending June; 30, 1968". (78 Stat. 1107; 79 Stat. 1254, 20 USC 591.)

(b) Such section is further amended by striking out the period at the end of clause (3) and inserting in lieu thereof a comma and the word "or", and by inserting after such clause a new clauses as follows (79 Stat. 1228.):

"(4) who are engaged in or preparing to engage in special educational programs for children of limited English-speaking ability."

Amendments to Cooperative Research Act
Sec. 706. Subsections (a) and (b) of section 2 of the Cooperative Research Act are each amended by inserting "and title VI after "section 503(a)(4)". (68 Stat. 533; 79 Stat. 44, 20 USC 331, note.)

Approved January 2, 1968

Appendix B

Public Law 93-380—Aug. 21, 1974
Strengthening State and Local Educational Agencies
Sec. 104. (a) Section 501(b) of the Elementary and Secondary Education Act of 1965 is amended by inserting before the period at the end thereof the following: "and each of the five succeeding fiscal years, except that no funds are authorized to be appropriated for obligation by the Commissioner during any year for which funds are available for obligation by the Commissioner for carrying out part C of title IV". (20 USC 861.)

(b) Section 521(b) of such Act is amended by inserting before the period at the end thereof the following: ", and each of the five succeeding fiscal years, except that no funds are authorized to be appropriated for obligation by the Commissioner during any year for which funds are available for obligation by the Commissioner for carrying out part C of title IV". (20 USC 868.)

(c) Section 531(b) of such Act is amended by inserting before the period at the end thereof the following: ", and each of the five succeeding fiscal years, except that no funds are authorized to be appropriated for obligation during any year for which funds are available for obligation for carrying out part C of title IV". (20 USC 867.)

(d) The amendments made by this section shall be effective on and after July 1, 1973. (Effective date, 20 USC 861, note.)

Bilingual Educational Programs
Sec. 105. (a)(1) Title VII of the Elementary and Secondary Education Act of 1965 is amended to read as follows (20 USC 880b.):

"Title VII—Bilingual Education
"Short Title
"Sec. 701. This title may be cited as the 'Bilingual Education Act'.

"Policy; Appropriations
"Sec. 702. (a) Recognizing (20 USC 880b.)—

"1. that there are large numbers of children of limited English-speaking ability;

"2. that many of such children have a cultural heritage which differs from that of English-speaking persons;

"3. that a primary means by which a child learns is through the use of such child's language and cultural heritage;

"4. that, therefore, large numbers of children of limited English-speaking ability have educational needs which can be met by the use of bilingual educational methods and techniques; and

"5. that, in addition, children of limited English-speaking ability benefit through the fullest utilization of multiple language and cultural resources.

the Congress declares it to be the policy of the United States, in order to establish equal educational opportunity for all children (A) to encourage the establishment and operation, where appropriate, of educational programs using bilingual educational practices, techniques, and methods, and (B) for that purpose, to provide financial assistance to local educational agencies, and to state educational agencies for certain purposes, in order to enable such local educational agencies to develop and carry out such programs in elementary and secondary schools, including activities at the preschool level, which are designed to meet the educational needs of such children; and to demonstrate effective ways of providing, for children of limited English-speaking ability, instruction designed to enable them, while using their native language, to achieve competence in the English language.

"(b)(1) Except as otherwise provided in this title, for the purpose of carrying out the provisions of this title, there are authorized to be appropriated $135,000,000 for the fiscal year ending June 30, 1974; $135,000,000 for the fiscal year ending June 30, 1975; $140,000,000 for the fiscal year ending June 30, 1976; $150,000,000 for the fiscal year ending June 30, 1977; and $160,000,000 for the fiscal year ending June 30, 1978. (Appropriation.)

"(2) There are further authorized to be appropriated to carry out the provisions of section 721(b)(3) $6,750,000 for the fiscal year ending June 30, 1974; $7,250,000 for the fiscal year ending June 30, 1975; $7,750,000 for the fiscal year ending June 30, 1976; $8,750,000 for the fiscal year ending June 30, 1977; and $9,750,000 for the fiscal year ending June 30, 1978. (Post, p. 506.)

"(A) the Commissioner shall reserve $16,000,000 of that part thereof which does not exceed $70,000,000 for training activities carried out under clause (3) of subsection (a) of section 721, and shall reserve for such activities 33-⅓ per centum of that part thereof which is in excess of $70,000,000; and

"(B) the Commissioner shall reserve from the amount not reserved pursuant to clause (A) of this paragraph such amounts as may be necessary, but not in excess of 1 per centum thereof, for the purposes of section 732. (Post, p. 510.)

"Definitions; Regulations

"Sec. 703. (a) The following definitions shall apply to the terms used in this title (20 USC 880b-1.):

"1. The term 'limited English-speaking ability', when used with reference to an individual, means—

"(A) individuals who were not born in the United States or whose native language is a language other than English, and

"(B) individuals who come from environments where a language other than English is dominant, as further defined by the Commissioner by regulations;

and, by reason thereof, have difficulty speaking and understanding instruction in the English language.

"2. The term 'native language', when used with reference to an individual of limited English-speaking ability, means the language normally used by such individuals, or in the case of a child, the language normally used by the parents of the child.

"3. The term 'low-income' when used with respect to a family means an annual income for such a family which does not exceed the low annual income determined pursuant to section 103 of title I of the Elementary and Secondary Education Act of 1965. (Ante, p. 488.)

"4. (A) The term 'program of bilingual education' means a program of instruction, designed for children of limited English-speaking ability in elementary or secondary schools, in which, with respect to the years of study to which such program is applicable—

> "(i) there is instruction given in, and study of, English and, to the extent necessary to allow a child to progress effectively through the educational system, the native language of the children of limited English-speaking ability, and such instruction is given with appreciation for the cultural heritage of such children, and, with respect to elementary school instruction, such instruction shall, to the extent necessary, be in all courses or subjects of study which will allow a child to progress effectively through the educational system; and

> "(ii) the requirements in subparagraphs (B) through (E) of this paragraph and established pursuant to subsection (b) of this section are met.

"(B) A program of bilingual education may make provision for the voluntary enrollment to a limited degree therein, on a regular basis of children whose language is English, in order that they may acquire an understanding of the cultural heritage of the children of limited English-speaking ability for whom the particular program of bilingual education is designed. In determining the eligibility to participate in such programs, priority shall be given to the children whose language is other than English. In no event shall the program be designed for the purpose of teaching a foreign language to English-speaking children. (English-speaking children, enrollment.)

"(C) In such courses or subjects of study as art, music, and physical education, a program of bilingual education shall make provision for the participation of children of limited English-speaking ability in regular classes.

"(D) Children enrolled in a program of bilingual education shall, if graded classes are used, be placed, to the extent practicable, in classes with children of approximately the same age and level of educational attainment. If children of significantly varying ages or levels of educational attainment are placed in the same class, the program of bilingual education shall seek to insure that each child is provided with instruction which is appropriate for his or her level of educational attainment.

"(E) An application for a program of bilingual education shall be developed in consultation with parents of children of limited English-speaking ability, teachers, and, where applicable, secondary school students, in the areas to be served, and assurances shall be given in the application that, after the application has been approved under this title, the applicant will provide for participation by a committee composed of, and selected by, such parents, and, in the case of secondary schools, representatives of secondary school students to be served. (Application.)

"5. The term 'Office' means the Office of Bilingual Education. (Definition.)

"6. The term 'Director' means the Director of the Office of Bilingual Education.

"7. The term 'Council' means the National Advisory Council on Bilingual Education.

"(b) The Commissioner, after receiving recommendations from State and local educational agencies and groups and organizations involved in bilingual education, shall establish, publish, and distribute, with respect to programs of bilingual education, suggested models with respect to pupil-teacher ratios, teacher qualifications, and other factors affecting the quality of instruction offered in such programs. (Models.)

"(c) In prescribing regulations under this section, the Commissioner shall consult with State and local educational agencies, appropriate organizations representing parents and children of limited English-speaking ability, and appropriate groups and organizations representing teachers and educators involved in bilingual education. (Consultations.)

"Part A—Financial Assistance for Bilingual Education Programs
"Bilingual Education Programs
"Sec. 721. (a) Funds available for grants under this part shall be used for (Grants, 20 USC 880b-7.)—

"1. the establishment, operation, and improvement of programs of bilingual education;

"2. auxiliary and supplementary community and educational activities designed to facilitate and expand the implementation of programs described in clause (1), including such activities as (A) adult education programs related to the purposes of this title, particularly for parents of children participating in programs of bilingual education, and carried out, where appropriate, in coordination with programs assisted under the Adult Education Act, and (B) preschool programs preparatory and supplementary to bilingual education programs (Post, p. 576, 20 USC 1201, note.);

"3. (A) the establishment, operation, and improvement of training programs for personnel preparing to participate in, or personnel participating in, the conduct of programs of bilingual education and (B) auxiliary and supplementary training programs, which shall be included in each program of bilingual education, for personnel preparing to participate in, or personnel participating in, the conduct of such programs; and

"4. planning, and providing technical assistance for, and taking other steps leading to the development of, such programs.

"(b)(1) A grant may be made under this section only upon application therefor by one or more local educational agencies or by an institution of higher education, including a junior or community college, applying jointly with one or more local educational agencies (or, in the case of a training activity described in clause (3)(A) of subsection (a) of this section, by eligible applicants as defined in section 723). Each such application shall be made to the Commissioner at such time, in such manner, and containing such information as the Commissioner deems necessary (Application.; Post, p. 508.), and

"(A) include a description of the activities set forth in one or more of the clauses of subsection (a) which the applicant desires to carry out; and

"(B) provide evidence that the activities so described will make substantial progress toward making programs of bilingual education available to the children having need thereof in the area served by the applicant.

"(2) An application for a grant under this part may be approved only if (Approval.)—

"(A) the provision of assistance proposed in the application is consistent with criteria established by the Commissioner, after consultation with the State educational agency, for the purpose of achieving an equitable distribution of assistance under this part within the State in which the applicant is located, which criteria shall be developed by his taking into consideration (i) the geographic distribution of children of limited English-speaking ability, (ii) the relative need of persons in different geographic areas within the State for the kinds of services and activities described in subsection (a), (iii) with respect to grants to carry out programs described in clauses (1) and (2) of subsection (a) of section 721, the relative ability of particular local educational agencies within the State to provide such services and activities, and (iv) with respect to such grants, the relative numbers of persons from low-income families sought to be benefitted by such programs;

"(B) in the case of applications from local educational agencies to carry out programs of bilingual education under clause (1) of subsection (a) of section 721, the Commissioner determines that not less than 15 per centum of the amounts paid to the applicant for the purposes of such programs shall be expended for auxiliary and supplementary training programs in accordance with the provisions of clause (3)(B) of such subsection and section 723 (Post, p. 508.);

"(C) the Commissioner determines (i) that the program will use the most qualified available personnel and the best resources and will substantively increase the educational opportunities for children of limited English-speaking ability in the area to be served by the applicant, and (ii) that, to the extent consistent with the number of children enrolled in nonprofit, nonpublic schools in the area to be served whose educational needs are of the type which the program is intended to meet, provision has been made for participation of such children; and

"(D) the State educational agency has been notified of the application and has been given the opportunity to offer recommendations thereon to the applicant and to the Commissioner.

"(3)(A) Upon an application from a State educational agency, the Commissioner shall make provision for the submission and approval of a State program for the coordination by such State agency of technical assistance to programs of bilingual education in such State assisted under this title. Such State program shall contain such provisions, agreements, and assurances as the Commissioner shall, by regulation, determine necessary and proper to achieve the purposes of this title, including assurances that funds made available under this section for any fiscal year will be so used as to supplement, and to the extent practical, increase the level of funds that would, in the absence of such funds be made available by the State for the purposes described in this section, and in no case to supplant such funds.

"(B) Except as is provided in the second sentence of this subparagraph, the Commissioner shall pay from the amounts authorized for these purposes pursuant to section 702 for each fiscal year to each State educational agency which has a State program submitted and approved under subparagraph (A) such sums as may be necessary for the proper and efficient conduct of such State program. The amount paid by the Commissioner to any State educational agency under the preceding sentence for any fiscal year shall not exceed 5 per centum of the aggregate of the amounts paid under this part to local educational agencies in the State of such State educational agency in the fiscal year preceding the fiscal year in which this limitation applies. (Ante, p. 503.)

"(c) In determining the distribution of funds under this title, the Commissioner shall give priority to areas having the greatest need for programs assisted under this title.

"Indian Children in Schools

"Sec. 722. (a) For the purpose of carrying out programs under this part for individuals served by elementary and secondary schools operated predominantly for Indian children, a nonprofit institution or organization of the Indian tribe concerned which operates any such school and which is approved by the Commissioner for the purposes of this section may be considered to be a local educational agency as such term is used in this title. (20 USC 880b-8.)

"(b) From the sums appropriated pursuant to section 702(b), the Commissioner is authorized to make payments to the Secretary of the Interior to carry out programs of bilingual education for children on reservations served by elementary and secondary schools for Indian children operated or funded by the Department of the Interior. The terms upon which payments for such purpose may be made to the Secretary of the Interior shall be determined pursuant to such criteria as the Commissioner determines will best carry out the policy of section 702(a). (Payments, Ante, p. 503.)

"(c) The Secretary of the Interior shall prepare and, not later than November 1 of each year, shall submit to the Congress and the President an annual report detailing a review and evaluation of the use, during the preceding fiscal year, of all funds paid to him by the Commissioner under subsection (b) of this section, including complete fiscal reports, a description of the personnel and information paid for in whole or in part with such funds, the allocation of such funds, and the status of all programs funded from such payments. Nothing in this subsection shall be construed to relieve the Director of any authority or obligation under this part. (Annual report to Congress and President.)

"(d) The Secretary of the Interior shall, together with the information required in the preceding subsection, submit to the Congress and the President, an assessment of the needs of Indian children with respect to the purposes of this title in schools operated or funded by the Department of the Interior, including those State educational agencies and local educational agencies receiving assistance under the Johnson-O'Malley Act (25 U.S.C. 452 et seq.) and an assessment to such schools for educational purposes through the Secretary of the Interior. (Assessment of needs of Indian children, submittal to Congress and President.)

"Training
"Sec. 723. (a)(1) In carrying out the provisions of clauses (1) and (3) of subsection (a) of section 721, with respect to training, the Commissioner shall, through grants to, and contracts with, eligible applicants, as defined in subsection (b), provide for (20 USC 880b-9, Ante, p. 506.)

"(A)(i) training, carried out in coordination with any other programs training auxiliary educational personnel, designed (I) to prepare personnel to participate in, or for personnel participating in, the conduct of programs of bilingual education, including programs emphasizing opportunities for career development, advancement, and lateral mobility, (II) to train teachers, administrators, para-professionals, teacher aides, and parents, and (III) to train persons to teach and counsel such persons, and (ii) special training programs designed (I) to meet individual needs, and (II) to encourage reform, innovation, and improvement in applicable education curricula in graduate education, in the structure of the academic profession, and in recruitment and retention of higher education and graduate school facilities, as related to bilingual education; and

"(B) the operation of short-term training institutes designed to improve the skills of participants in programs of bilingual education in order to facilitate their effectiveness in carrying out responsibilities in connection with such programs.

"(2) In addition the Commissioner is authorized to award fellowships for study in the field of training teachers for bilingual education. For the fiscal year ending June 30, 1975, not less than 100 fellowships leading to a graduate degree shall be awarded under the preceding sentence for preparing individuals to train teachers for programs of bilingual education. Such fellowships shall be awarded in proportion to the need for teachers of various groups of individuals with limited English-speaking ability. For each fiscal year after June 30, 1975, and prior to July 1, 1978, the Commissioner shall report to the Committee on Education and Labor of the House of Representatives and the Committee on Labor and Public Welfare of the Senate on the number of fellowships in the field of training teachers for bilingual education which he recommends will be necessary for that fiscal year. (Fellowships; Report to congressional committees.)

"(3) The Commissioner shall include in the terms of any arrangement described in paragraphs (1) and (2) of subsection (a) of this section provisions for the payment, to persons participating in training programs so described, of such stipends (including allowances for subsistence and other expenses for such persons and their dependents) as he may determine to be consistent with prevailing practices under comparable federally supported programs. (Stipends.)

"(4) In making grants or contracts under this section, the Commissioner shall give priority to eligible applicants with demonstrated competence and experience in the field of bilingual education. Funds provided under grants or contracts for training activities described in this section to or with a State educational agency, separately or jointly, shall in no event exceed in the aggregate in any fiscal year 15 per centum of the total amount of funds obligated for training activities pursuant to clauses (1) and (3) of subsection (a) of section 721 in such year. (Ante, p. 506.)

"(5) An application for a grant or contract for preservice or inservice training activities described in clause (A)(i)(I) and clause (A)(ii)(I) and in subsection (a)(1)(B) of this section shall be considered an application for a program of bilingual education for the purposes of subsection (a)(4)(E) of section 703. (Ante, p. 504.)

"(b) For the purposes of this section, the term 'eligible applicants' means (:Eligible applicants.")—

"(1) institutions of higher education (including junior colleges and community colleges) which apply, after consultation with, or jointly with, one or more local educational agencies;

"(2) local educational agencies; and

"(3) State educational agencies.

"Part B—Administration
"Office of Bilingual Education

"Sec. 731. (a) There shall be, in the Office of Education, an Office of Bilingual Education (hereafter in this section referred to as the 'Office') through which the Commissioner shall carry out his functions relating to bilingual education. (Establishment, 20 USC 880b-10.)

"(b)(1) The Office shall be headed by a Director of Bilingual Education, appointed by the Commissioner, to whom the Commissioner shall delegate all of his delegable functions relating to bilingual education.

"(2) The Office shall be organized as the Director determines to be appropriate in order to enable him to carry out his functions and responsibilities effectively.

"(c) The Commissioner, in consultation with the Council, shall prepare and, not later than November 1 of 1975, and of 1977, shall submit to the Congress and the President a report on the condition of bilingual education in the Nation and the administration and operation of this title and of other programs for persons of limited English-speaking ability. Such report shall include (Report to Congress and President; Contents.)—

"(1) a national assessment of the educational needs of children and other persons with limited English-speaking ability and of the extent to which such needs are being met from Federal, State, and local efforts, including (A) not later than July 1, 1977, the results of a survey of the number of such children and persons in the State, and (B) a plan, including cost estimates, to be carried out during the five-year period beginning on such date, for extending programs of bilingual education and bilingual vocational and adult education programs to all such preschool and elementary school children and other persons of limited English-speaking ability, including a phased plan for the training of the necessary teachers and other educational personnel necessary for such purpose;

"(2) a report on and an evaluation of the activities carried out under this title during the preceding fiscal year and the extent to which each of such activities achieves the policy set forth in section 702(a);

"(3) a statement of the activities intended to be carried out during the succeeding period, including an estimate of the cost of such activities;

"(4) an assessment of the number of teachers and other educational personnel needed to carry out programs of bilingual education under this title and those carried out under other programs for persons of limited English-speaking ability and a statement describing the activities carried out thereunder designed to prepare teachers and other educational personnel needed to carry out programs of bilingual education in the States and a statement describing the activities carried out under this title designed to prepare teachers and other educational personnel for such programs; and

"(5) a description of the personnel, the functions of such personnel, and information available at the regional offices of the Department of Health, Education, and Welfare dealing with bilingual programs within the region.

"National Advisory Council on Bilingual Education

"Sec. 732. (a) Subject to part I) of the General Education Provisions Act, there shall be a National Advisory Council on Bilingual Education composed of fifteen members appointed by the Secretary, one of whom he shall designate as Chairman. At least eight of the members of the Council shall be persons experienced in dealing with the educational problems of children and other persons who are of limited English-speaking ability, at least one of whom shall be representative of persons serving on boards of education operating programs of bilingual education. At least three members shall be experienced in the training of teachers in programs of bilingual education. At least two members shall be persons with general experience in the field of elementary and secondary education. At least two members shall be classroom teachers of demonstrated teaching abilities using bilingual methods and techniques. The members of the Council shall be appointed in such a way as to be generally representative of the significant segments of the population of persons of limited English-speaking ability and the geographic areas in which they reside. (Establishment, 20 USC 880b-11, Post, p. 575; Membership.)

(b) The Council shall meet at the call of the Chairman, but, notwithstanding the provisions of section 446(a) of the General Education Provisions Act, not less often than four times in each year. (20 USC 1233e, Duties.)

"(c) The Council shall advise the Commissioner in the preparation of general regulations and with respect to policy matters arising in the administration and operation of this title, including the development of criteria for approval of applications, and plans under this title, and the administration and operation of other programs for persons of limited English-speaking ability. The Council shall prepare and, not later than November 1 of each year, submit a report to the Congress and the President on the condition of bilingual education in the Nation and on the administration and operation of this title, including those items specified in section 731(c), and the administration and operation of other programs for persons of limited English-speaking ability. (Report to Congress and President, Ante, p. 509.)

"(d) The Commissioner shall procure temporary and intermittent services of such personnel as are necessary for the conduct of the functions of the Council, in accordance with section 445, of the General Education Provisions Act, and shall make available to the Council such staff, information, and other assistance as it may require to carry out its activities effectively. (20 USC 1233d.)

"Part C—Supportive Services and Activities
"Administration

"Sec. 741. (a) The provisions of this part shall be administered by the Assistant Secretary, in consultation with (20 USC 880b-12.)—

"1. the Commissioner, through the Office of Bilingual Education (20 USC 1225.); and

"2. the Director of the National Institute of Education, notwithstanding the second sentence of section 405(b)(1) of the General Education Provisions Act;

in accordance with regulations. (Regulations.)

"(b) The Assistant Secretary shall, in accordance with clauses (1) and (2) of subsection (a), develop and promulgate regulations for this part and then delegate his functions under this part, as may be appropriate under the terms of section 742. (Infra.)

"Research and Demonstration Projects

"Sec. 742. (a) The National Institute of Education shall, in accordance with the provisions of section 405 of the General Education Provisions Act, carry out a program of research in the field of bilingual education in order to enhance the effectiveness of bilingual education programs carried out under this title and other programs for persons of limited English-speaking ability. (Bilingual education research, 20 USC 880b-13, 20 USC 1221e.)

"(b) In order to test the effectiveness of research findings by the National Institute of Education and to demonstrate new or innovative practices, techniques, and methods for use in such bilingual education programs, the Director and the Commissioner are authorized to make competitive contracts with public and private educational agencies, institutions, and organizations for such purpose.

"(c) In carrying out their responsibilities under this section, the Commissioner and the Director shall, through competitive contracts with appropriate public and private agencies, institutions, and organizations—

"1. undertake studies to determine the basic educational needs and language acquisition characteristics of, and the most effective conditions for, educating children of limited English-speaking ability;

"2. develop and disseminate instructional materials and equipment suitable for use in bilingual education programs; and

"3. establish and operate a national clearinghouse of information for bilingual education, which shall collect, analyze, and disseminate information about bilingual education and such bilingual education and related programs.

"(d) In carrying out their responsibilities under this section, the Commissioner and the Director shall provide for periodic consultation with representatives of State and local educational agencies and appropriate groups and organizations involved in bilingual education.

"(e) There is authorized to be appropriated for each fiscal year prior to July 1, 1978, $5,000,000 to carry out the provisions of this section." (Appropriations.)

(2)(A) The amendment made by this subsection shall be effective upon the date of enactment of this Act, except that the provisions of part A of title VII of the Elementary and Secondary Education Act of 1965 (as amended by subsection (a) of this section) shall become effective on July 1, 1975, and the provisions of title VII of the Elementary and Secondary Education Act of 1965 in effect immediately prior to the date of enactment of this Act shall remain in effect through June 30, 1975, to the extent not inconsistent with the amendment made by this section. (Effective date, 20 USC 880b note.; Ante, p. 504, 20 USC 880b.)

(B) The National Advisory Council on Bilingual Education, for which provision is made in section 732 of such Act, shall be appointed within ninety days after the enactment of this Act.

(b) Section 703(a) of title VII of such Act is amended by adding at the end thereof the following (20 USC 880b–11 note.; Ante, p. 510, Other programs for persons of limited English-speaking ability."; Ante, p. 504.):

"(8) The term 'other programs for persons of limited English-speaking ability' when used in sections 731 and 732 means the program authorized by section 708(c) of the Emergency School Aid Act and the programs carried out in coordination with the provisions of this title pursuant to section 122(a)(4)(C) and part J of the Vocational Education Act of 1963, and section 306(a)(11) of the Adult Education Act, and programs and projects serving areas with high concentrations of persons of limited English-speaking ability pursuant to section 6(b)(4) of the Library Services and Construction Act.". (20 USC 1607. Post, p. 578. Post, p. 607. Post, p. 609.)

Statute of Limitations
Sec. 106. Title VIII of the Elementary and Secondary Education Act of 1965 is amended by inserting after section 803 the following new section (20 USC 881.):

"Statute of Limitations on Refund of Payments
"Sec. 804. No State or local educational agency shall be liable to refund any payment made to such agency under this Act (including title I of this Act) which was subsequently determined to be unauthorized by law, if such payment was made more than five years before such agency received final written notice that such payment was unauthorized.". (20 USC 884. Ante, p. 488.)

Dropout Prevention Projects
Sec. 107. (a) Section 807(c) of the Elementary and Secondary Education Act

of 1965 is amended by inserting before the period at the end thereof the following: ", and each of the five succeeding fiscal years, except that no funds are authorized to be appropriated for obligation during any year for which funds are available for obligation for carrying out part C of title IV". (20 USC 887.)

(b) The amendments made by this section shall be effective on and after July 1, 1973. (Effective date. 20 USC 887 note.)

School Nutrition and Health Services

Sec. 108. (a) Section 808(d) of the Elementary and Secondary Education Act of 1965 is amended by inserting before the period at the end thereof the following: ", and each of the five succeeding fiscal years, except that no funds are authorized to be appropriated for obligation during any year for which funds are available for obligation for carrying out part C of title IV". (20 USC 887a.)

(b) The amendments made by this section shall be effective on and after July 1, 1973. (Effective date. 20 USC 887b note.)

Correction Education Services

Sec. 109. (a) Section 809 of the Elementary and Secondary Education Act of 1965 is amended by adding at the end thereof the following new subsection (20 USC 887b.):

"(c) For the purpose of carrying out this section, there is authorized to be appropriated $500,000 for the fiscal year ending June 30, 1974, and for the succeeding fiscal year."

(b) The amendments made by this section shall be effective on and after July 1, 1974. (Effective date. 20 USC 887b note.)

Open Meeting of Educational Agencies

Sec. 110. Title VIII of the Elementary and Secondary Education Act of 1965 is amended by adding at the end thereof the following new section:

"Open Meetings of Educational Agencies

"Sec. 812. No application for assistance under this Act may be considered unless the local educational agency making such application certifies to the Commissioner that members of the public have been afforded the opportunity upon reasonable notice to testify or otherwise comment regarding the subject matter of the application. The Commissioner is authorized and directed to establish such regulations as necessary to implement this section." (20 USC 887e.)

Ethnic Heritage Studies Centers
Sec. 111. (a)(1) Section 907 of the Elementary and Secondary Education Act of 1965 is amended by striking out "the fiscal year ending June 30, 1973" and inserting in lieu thereof "each of the fiscal years ending prior to July 1, 1978". (20 USC 900a-5.)

(2) The amendments made by this subsection shall be effective on and after July 1, 1973. (Effective date. 20 USC 900a-5 note.; 20 USC 900a-1.)

(b) Section 903 of such Act is amended by—

1. striking out "elementary and secondary schools and institutions of higher education" in clause (1) of such section, and inserting in lieu thereof "elementary or secondary schools or institutions of higher education";

2. striking out "elementary and secondary schools and institutions of higher education" in clause (2) of such section and inserting in lieu thereof "elementary or secondary schools or institutions of higher education";

3. inserting the word "or" after clause (1) of such section (20 USC 900a-1); and

4. inserting the word "or" at the end of clause (2) of such section.

Title II—Equal Educational Opportunities and the Transportation of Students (Equal Educational Opportunities Act of 1974)
Short Title
Sec. 201. This title may be cited as the "Equal Educational Opportunities Act of 1974". (20 USC 1701 note.)

Part A—Equal Educational Opportunities
Subpart I—Policy and Purpose

Declaration of Policy
Sec. 202. (a) The Congress declares it to be the policy of the United States that (20 USC 1701)—

1. all children enrolled in public schools are entitled to equal educational opportunity without regard to race, color, sex, or national origin; and

2. the neighborhood is the appropriate basis for determining public school assignments.

(b) In order to carry out this policy, it is the purpose of this part to specify appropriate remedies for the orderly removal of the vestiges of the dual school system.

Findings
Sec. 203. (a) The Congress finds that (20 USC 1702.)—

1. the maintenance of dual school systems in which students are assigned to schools solely on the basis of race, color, sex, or national origin denies to those students the equal protection of the laws guaranteed by the fourteenth amendment;

2 for the purposes of abolishing dual school systems and eliminating the vestiges thereof, many local educational agencies have been required to reorganize their school systems, to reassign students, and to engage in the extensive transportation of students;

3. the implementation of desegregation plans that require extensive student transportation has, in many cases, required local educational agencies to expend large amounts of funds, thereby depleting their financial resources available for the maintenance or improvement of the quality of educational facilities and instruction provided;

4. transportation of students which creates serious risks to their health

and safety, disrupts the educational process carried out with respect to such students, and impinges significantly on their educational opportunity, is excessive;

5. the risks and harms created by excessive transportation are particularly great for children enrolled in the first six grades; and

6. the guidelines provided by the courts for fashioning remedies to dismantle dual school systems have been, as the Supreme Court of the United States has said, "incomplete and imperfect," and have not established, a clear, rational, and uniform standard for determining the extent to which a local educational agency is required to reassign and transport its students in order to eliminate the vestiges of a dual school system.

Appendix C

LAU v. NICHOLS

Syllabus

LAU ET AL v. NICHOLS ET AL

Certiorari to the United States Court
of Appeals for the Ninth Circuit

No. 72-6520. Argued December 10, 1973—Decided January 21, 1974

The failure of the San Francisco school system to provide English language instruction to approximately 1,800 students of Chinese ancestry who do not speak English, or to provide them with other adequate instructional procedures, denies them a meaningful opportunity to participate in the public educational program and thus violates §601 of the Civil Rights Act of 1964, which bans discrimination based "on the ground of race, color, or national origin," in "any program or activity receiving Federal financial assistance," and the implementing regulations of the Department of Health, Education, and Welfare. Pp. 565-569.

483 F.2d 791, reversed and remanded.

Douglas, J., delivered the opinion of the Court, in which Brennan, Marshall, Powell, and Rehnquist, J., joined. Stewart, J., filed an opinion concurring in the result, in which Burger, C.J., and Blackmun, J., joined, post, p. 569. White, J., concurred in the result. Blackmun, J., filed an opinion concurring in the result, in which Burger, C.J., joined, post, p. 571.

Edward H. Steinman argued the cause for petitioners. With him on the briefs were Kenneth Hecht and David C. Moon.

Thomas M. O'Connor argued the cause for respondents. With him on the brief were George E. Krueger and Burk E. Delventhal.

Assistant Attorney General Pottinger argued the cause for the United States as amicus curiae urging reversal. With him on the brief were Solicitor General Bork, Deputy Solicitor General Wallace, Mark L. Evans, and Brian K. Landsberg.*

MR. JUSTICE DOUGLAS delivered the opinion of the Court.

The San Francisco, California, school system was integrated in 1971 as a result of a federal court decree, 339 F. Supp. 1315. See Lee v. Johnson, 404 U.S. 1215. The District Court found that there are 2,856 students of Chinese ancestry in the school system who do not speak English. Of those who have that language deficiency, about 1,000 are given supplemental courses in the English language.[1] About 1,800, however, do not receive that instruction.

This class suit brought by non-English-speaking Chinese students against officials responsible for the operation of the San Francisco Unified School District seeks relief against the unequal educational opportunities, which are alleged to violate, inter alia, the Fourteenth Amendment. No specific remedy is urged upon us. Teaching English to the students of Chinese ancestry who do not speak the language is one choice. Giving instructions to this group in Chinese is another. There may be others. Petitioners ask only that the Board of Education be directed to apply its expertise to the problem and rectify the situation.

The District Court denied relief. The Court of Appeals affirmed, holding that there was no violation of the Equal Protection Clause of the Fourteenth Amendment or of §601 of the Civil Rights Act of 1964, 78 Stat. 252, 42 U.S.C. §2000d, which excludes from participation in federal financial assistance, recipients of aid which discriminate against racial groups, 483 F.2d 791. One judge dissented. A hearing en banc was denied, two judges dissenting. Id., at 805.

We granted the petition for certiorari because of the public importance of the question presented, 412 U.S. 938.

The Court of Appeals reasoned that "[e]very student brings to the starting line of his educational career different advantages and disadvantages caused in part by social, economic and cultural background, created and continued completely apart from any contribution by the school system," 483 F.2d, at 797. Yet in our view the case may not be so easily decided. This is a public school system of California and §71 of the California Education Code states that "English shall be the basic language of instruction in all schools." That section permits a school district to determine "when and under what circumstances instruction may be given bilingually." That section also states as "the policy of the state" to insure "the mastery of English by all pupils in the schools." And bilingual instruction is authorized "to the extent that it does not interfere with the systematic, sequential, and regular instruction of all pupils in the English language."

Moreover, §8573 of the Education Code provides that no pupil shall receive a diploma of graduation from grade 12 who has not met the standards of proficiency in "English," as well as other prescribed subjects. Moreover, by §12101 of the Education Code (Supp. 1973) children between the ages of six and 16 years are (with exceptions not material here) "subject to compulsory full-time education."

Under these state-imposed standards there is no equality of treatment merely by providing students with the same facilities, textbooks, teachers, and curriculum; for students who do not understand English are effectively foreclosed from any meaningful education.

Basic English skills are at the very core of what these public schools teach. Imposition of a requirement that, before a child can effectively participate in the educational program, he must already have acquired those basic skills is to make a mockery of public education. We know that those who do not understand English are certain to find their classroom experiences wholly incomprehensible and in no way meaningful.

We do not reach the Equal Protection Clause argument which has been advanced but rely solely on §601 of the Civil Rights Act of 1964, 42 U.S.C. §2000d, to reverse the Court of Appeals.

That section bans discrimination based "on the grounds of race, color, or national origin," in "any program or activity receiving Federal financial assistance." The school district involved in this litigation receives large amounts of federal financial assistance. The Department of Health, Education, and Welfare (HEW), which has authority to promulgate regulations prohibiting discrimination in federally assisted school systems, 42 U.S.C. §2000d-1, in 1968 issued one guideline that "[s]chool systems are responsible for assuring that students of a particular race, color, or national origin are not denied the opportunity to obtain the education generally obtained by other students in the system." 33 Fed. Reg. 4956. In 1970 HEW made the guidelines more specific, requiring school districts that were federally funded "to rectify the language deficiency in order to open" the instruction to students who had "linguistic deficiencies," 35 Fed. Reg. 11595.

By §602 of the Act HEW is authorized to issue rules, regulations, and orders[2] to make sure that recipients of federal aid under its jurisdiction conduct any federally financed projects consistently with §601. HEW's regulations, 45 CFR §80.3(b)(1), specify that the recipients may not

> "(ii) Provide any service, financial aid, or other benefit to an individual which is different, or is provided in a different manner, from that provided to others under the program;

> "(iv) Restrict an individual in any way in the enjoyment of any advantage or privilege enjoyed by others receiving any service, financial aid, or other benefit under the program."

Discrimination among students on account of race or national origin that is prohibited includes "discrimination...in the availability or use of any academic...or other facilities of the grantee or other recipient." Id., §80.5(b).

Discrimination is barred which has that effect even though no purposeful design is present: a recipient "may not...utilize criteria or methods of administration which have the effect of subjecting individuals to discrimination" or have "the effect of defeating or substantially impairing accomplishment of the objectives of the program as respect individuals of a particular race, color, or national origin." Id., §80.3(b)(2).

It seems obvious that the Chinese-speaking minority receives fewer benefits than the English-speaking majority from respondents' school systems which denies them a meaningful opportunity to participate in the educational program–all earmarks of the discrimination banned by the regulations.[3] In 1970 HEW issued clarifying guidelines, 35 Fed. Reg. 11595, which include the following:

"Where inability to speak and understand the English language excludes national origin-minority group children from effective participation in the educational program offered by a school district, the district must take affirmative steps to rectify the language deficiency in order to open its instructional program to these students."

"Any ability grouping or tracking system employed by the school system to deal with the special language skill needs of national origin-minority group children must be designed to meet such language skill needs as soon as possible and must not operate as an educational deadend or permanent track."

Respondent school district contractually agreed to "comply with title VI of the Civil Rights Act of 1964...and all requirements imposed by or pursuant to the Regulation" of HEW (45 CFR pt. 80) which are "issued pursuant to that tiel..." and also immediately to "take any measures necessary to effectuate this agreement." The Federal Government has power to fix the terms on which its money allotments to the States shall be disbursed. Oklahoma v. CSC, 330 U.S.s 127, 142–143. Whatever may be the limits of that power, Steward Machine Co. v. Davis, 301 U.S. 548, 590 et seq., they have not been reached here. Senator Humphrey, during the floor debates on the Civil Rights Act of 1964, said:[4]

"Simple justice requires that public funds, to which all taxpayers of all races contribute, not be spent in any fashion which encourages, entrenches, subsidizes, or results racial discrimination."

We accordingly reverse the judgment of the Court of Appeals and remand the case for the fashioning of appropriate relief.

Reversed and remanded.

Mr. Justice White concurs in the result.

Mr. Justice Stewart, with whom The Chief Justice and Mr. Justice Blackmun join, concurring in the result.

It is uncontested that more than 2,800 school children of Chinese ancestry attend school in the San Francisco Unified School District system even though they do not speak, understand, read, or write the English language, and that as to some 1,800 of these pupils the respondent school authorities have taken no significant steps to deal with this language deficiency. The petitioners do not contend, however, that the respondents have affirmatively or intentionally contributed to this inadequacy, but only that they have failed to act in the face of changing social and linguistic patterns. Because of this laissez-faire attitude on the part of the school administrators, it is not entirely clear that §601 of the Civil Rights Act of 1964, 42 U.S.C. §2000d, standing alone, would render illegal the expenditure of federal funds on these schools. For that section provides that "[n]o person in the United States shall, on the ground of race, color, or national origin, be excluded from participation in, be denied the benefits of, or be subjected to discrimination under any program or activity receiving Federal financial assistance."

On the other hand, the interpretive guidelines published by the Office for Civil Rights of the Department of Health, Education, and Welfare in 1970, 35 Fed. Reg. 11595, clearly indicate that affirmative efforts to give special training for non-English-speaking pupils are required by Tit. VI as a condition to receipt of federal aid to public schools:

> "Where inability to speak and understand the English language excludes national origin-minority group children from effective participation in the educational program offered by a school district, the district must take affirmative steps to rectify the language deficiency in order to open its instructional program to these students."[5]

35 Fed. Reg. 11595.

The critical question is, therefore, whether the regulations and guidelines promulgated by HEW go beyond the authority of §601.[6] Last Term, in Mourning v. Family Publications Service, Inc., 411 U.S. 356, 369, we held that the validity of a regulation promulgated under a general authorization provision such as §602 of Tit. VI[7] "will be sustained so long as it is 'reasonably related to the purposes of the enabling legislation.' Thorpe v. Housing Authority of the City of Durham, 393 U.S. 268, 280-281 (1969)." I think the guidelines here fairly meet that test. Moreover, in assessing the purposes of remedial legislation we have found that departmental regulations and "consistent administrative construction" are "entitled to great weight." Trafficante v. Metropolitan Life Insurance Co., 409 U.S. 205, 210; Griggs v. Duke Power Co., 401 U.S. 424, 433–434; Udall v. Tallman, 380 U.S. 1. The Department has reasonably and consistently interpreted §601 to require affirmative remedial efforts to give special attention to linguistically deprived children.

For these reasons I concur in the result reached by the Court.

Mr. Justice Blackmun, with whom The Chief Justice joins, concurring in the result.

I join Mr. Justice Stewart's opinion and thus I, too concur in the result. Against the possibility that the Court's judgment may be interpreted too broadly, I stress the fact that the children with whom we are concerned here number about 1,800. This is a very substantial group that is being deprived of any meaningful schooling because they cannot understand the language of the classroom. We may only guess as to why they have had no exposure to English in their preschool years. Earlier generations of American ethnic groups have overcome the language barrier by earnest parental endeavor or by the hard fact of being pushed out of the family or community nest and into the realities of broader experience.

I merely wish to make plain that when, in another case, we are concerned with a very few youngsters, or with just a single child who speaks only German or Polish or Spanish or any language other than English, I would not regard today's decision, or the separate concurrence, as conclusive upon the issue whether the statute and the guideline require the funded school district to provide special instruction. For me, numbers are at the heart of this case and my concurrence is to be understood accordingly.

Appendix D

BROWN v. BOARD OF EDUCATION

Syllabus

BROWN ET AL. v. BOARD OF EDUCATION OF TOPEKA ET AL.

No. 1. APPEAL FROM THE UNITED STATES DISTRICT COURT FOR THE DISTRICT OF KANSAS.*

Argued December 9, 1952,—Reargued December 8, 1953.—
Decided May 17, 1954.

Segregation of white and Negro children in the public schools of a State solely on the basis of race, pursuant to state laws permitting or requiring such segregation, denies to Negro children the equal protection of the laws guaranteed by the Fourteenth Amendment–even though the physical facilities and other "tangible" factors of white and Negro schools may be equal. Pp. 486–496.

(a) The history of the Fourteenth Amendment is inconclusive as to its intended effect on public education. Pp. 489–490.

(b) The question presented in these cases must be determined, not on the basis of conditions existing when the Fourteenth Amendment was adopted, but in the light of the full development of public education and its present place in American life throughout the Nation. Pp. 492–493.

(c) Where a State has undertaken to provide an opportunity for an education in its public schools, such an opportunity is a right which must be made available to all on equal terms. P. 493.

(d) Segregation of children in public schools solely on the basis of race deprives children of the minority group of equal educational opportunities, even though the physical facilities and other "tangible" factors may be equal. Pp.493–494.

(e) The "separate but equal" doctrine adopted in Plessy v. Ferguson, 163 U.S. 537, has no place in the field of public education. P. 495.

(f) The cases are restored to the docket for further argument on specified questions relating to the forms of the decrees. Pp. 495-496.

Robert L. Carter argued the cause for appellants in No. 1 on the original argument and on the reargument. Thurgood Marshall argued the cause for appellants in No. 2 on the original argument and Spottswood W. Robinson, III, for appellants in No. 4 on the original argument, and both argued the causes for appellants in Nos. 2 and 4 on the reargument. Louis L. Redding and Jack Greenberg argued the cause for respondents in No. 10 on the original argument and Jack Greenberg and Thurgood Marshall on the reargument.

On the briefs were Robert L. Carter, Thurgood Marshall, Spottswood W. Robinson, III, Louis L. Redding, Jack Greenberg, George E.C. Hayes, William R. Ming, Jr., Constance Baker Motley, James M. Nabrit, Jr., Charles S. Scott, Frank D. Reeves, Harold R. Boulware and Oliver W. Hill for appellants in Nos. 1, 2, and 4 and respondents in No. 10; George M. Johnson for appellants in Nos. 2 and 4. Arthur D. Shores and A.T. Walden were on the Statement as to Jurisdiction and a brief opposing a Motion to Dismiss or Affirm in No. 2.

Paul E. Wilson, Assistant Attorney General of Kansas, argued the cause for appellees in No. 1 on the original argument and on the reargument. With him on the briefs was Harold R. Fatzer, Attorney General.

John W. Davis argued the cause for appellees in No. 2 on the original argument and for appellees in Nos. 2 and 4 on the reargument. With him on the briefs in No. 2 were T.C. Callison, Attorney General of South Carolina, Robert McC. Figg, Jr., S.E. Rogers, William R. Meagher, and Taggart Whipple.

J. Lindsay Almond, Jr., Attorney General of Virginia, and T. Justin Moore argued the cause for appellees in No. 4 on the original argument and for appellees in Nos. 2 and 4 on the reargument. On the briefs in No. 4 were J. Lindsay Almond, Jr., Attorney General, and Henry T. Wickham, Special

Assistant Attorney General, for the State of Virginia, and T. Justin Moore, Archibald G. Robertson, John W. Riely, and T. Justin Moore, Jr. for the Prince Edward County School Authorities, appellees.

H. Albert Young, Attorney General of Delaware, argued the cause for petitioners in No. 10 on the original argument and on the reargument. With him on the briefs was Louis J. Finger, Special Deputy Attorney General.

By special leave of Court, Assistant Attorney General Rankin argued the cause for the United States on the reargument, as amicus curiae, urging reversal in Nos. 1, 2, and 4 and affirmance in No. 10. With him on the brief were Attorney General Brownell, Philip Elman, Leon Ulman, William J. Lamont, and M. Magdelena Schoch. James P. McGranery, then Attorney General, and Philip Elman filed a brief for the United States on the original argument, as amicus curiae, urging reversal in Nos. 1, 2, and 4 and affirmance in No. 10.

Briefs of amici curiae supporting appellants in No. 1 were filed by Shad Polier, Will Maslow, and Joseph B. Robison for the American Jewish Congress; by Edwin J. Lukas, Arnold Forster, Arthur Garfield Hays, Frank E. Karelsen, Leonard Haas, Saburo Kido, and Theodore Leskes for the American Civil Liberties Union et al.; and by John Ligtenberg and Selma M. Borchardt for the American Federation of Teachers. Briefs of amici curiae supporting appellants in No. 1 and respondents in No. 10 were filed by Arthur J. Goldberg and Thomas E. Harris for the Congress of Industrial Organizations and by Phineas Indritz for the American Veterans Committee, Inc.

Mr. Chief Justice Warren delivered the opinion of the Court.

These cases come to us from the States of Kansas, South Carolina, Virginia, and Delaware. They are premised on different facts and different local conditions, but a common legal question justifies their consideration together in this consolidated opinion.[1]

In each of these cases, minors of the Negro race, through their legal representatives, seek the aid of the courts in obtaining admission to the public schools of their community on a nonsegregated basis. In each instance, they had been denied admission to white schools attended by white children under laws requiring or permitting segregation according to race. This segregation was alleged to deprive the plaintiffs of the equal protection of the laws under the Fourteenth Amendment. In each of the cases other than the Delaware case, a three-judge federal district court denied relief to the plaintiffs on the so-called "separate but equal" doctrine announced by this Court in Plessy v. Ferguson, 163 U.S. 537. Under that doctrine, equality of treatment is accorded when the races are provided substantially equal facilities, even though these facilities be separate. In the Delaware case, the Supreme Court of Delaware adhered to that doctrine, but ordered that the plaintiffs be admitted to the white schools because of their superiority to the Negro schools.

The plaintiffs contend that segregated public schools are not "equal" and cannot be made "equal," and that hence they are deprived of the equal protection of the laws. Because of the obvious importance of the question presented, the Court took jurisdiction.[2] Argument was heard in the 1952 Term, and reargument was heard this Term on certain questions propounded by the Court.[3]

Reargument was largely devoted to the circumstances surrounding the adoption of the Fourteenth Amendment in 1868. It covered exhaustively consideration of the Amendment in Congress, ratification by the states, then existing practices in racial segregation, and the views of proponents and opponents of the Amendment. This discussion and our own investigation convince us that, although these sources cast some light, it is not enough to resolve the problem with which we are faced. At best, they are inconclusive. The most avid proponents of the post-War Amendments undoubtedly intended them to remove all legal distinctions among "all persons born or naturalized in the United States." Their opponents, just as certainly, were antagonistic to both the letter and the spirit of the Amendments and wished them to have the most limited effect. What others in Congress and the state legislatures had in mind cannot be determined with any degree of certainty.

An additional reason for the inconclusive nature of the Amendment's history, with respect to segregated schools, is the status of public education at that time.[4] In the South, the movement toward free common schools, supported by general taxation, had not yet taken hold. Education of white children was largely in the hands of private groups. Education of Negroes was almost nonexistent, and practically all of the race were illiterate. In fact, any education of Negroes was forbidden by law in some states. Today, in contrast, many Negroes have achieved outstanding success in the arts and sciences as well as in the business and professional world. It is true that public school education at the time of the Amendment had advanced further in the North, but the effect of the Amendment on Northern States was generally ignored in the congressional debates. Even in the North, the conditions of public education did not approximate those existing today. The curriculum was usually rudimentary; ungraded schools were common in rural areas; the school term was but three months a year in many states; and compulsory school attendance was virtually unknown. As a consequence, it is not surprising that there should be so little in the history of the Fourteenth Amendment relating to its intended effect on public education.

In the first cases in this Court construing the Fourteenth Amendment, decided shortly after its adoption the Court interpreted it as proscribing all state-imposed discriminations against the Negro race.[5] The doctrine of "separate but equal" did not make its appearance in this Court until 1896 in the case of Plessy v. Ferguson, supra, involving not education but transportation.[6] American courts have since labored with the doctrine for over half a century. In this Court, there have been six cases involving the "separate but equal" doctrine in the field of public education.[7] In Cumming v. County Board of Education, 175 U.S. 528, and Gong Lum v. Rice, 275 U.S. 78, the validity of the doctrine itself was not challenged.[8] In more recent cases, all on the graduate school level, inequality was found in that specific benefits enjoyed by white students were denied to Negro students of the same educational qualifications. Missouri ex rel. Gaines v. Canada, 305 U.S. 337; Sipuel v. Oklahoma, 332 U.S. 631; Sweatt v. Painter, 339 U.S. 629; McLaurin v. Oklahoma State Regents, 339 U.S. 637. In none of these cases was it necessary to re-examine the doctrine to grant relief to the Negro plaintiff. And in Sweatt v. Painter, supra, the Court expressly reserved decision on the question whether Plessy v. Ferguson should be held inapplicable to public education.

In the instant cases, that question is directly presented. Here, unlike Sweatt v. Painter, there are findings below that the Negro and white schools involved have been equalized, or are being equalized, with respect to buildings, curricula, qualifications and salaries of teachers, and other "tangible" factors.[9] "Our decision, therefore, cannot turn on merely a comparison of these tangible factors in the Negro and white schools involved in each of the cases. We must look instead to the effect of segregation itself on public education."

In approaching this problem, we cannot turn the clock back to 1868 when the Amendment was adopted, or even to 1896 when Plessy v. Ferguson was written. "We must consider public education in the light of its full development and its present place in American life throughout the Nation. Only in this way can it be determined if segregation in public schools deprives these plaintiffs of the equal protection of the laws.

Today, education is perhaps the most important function of state and local governments. Compulsory school attendance laws and the great expenditures for education both demonstrate our recognition of the importance of education to our democratic society. It is required in the performance of our most basic public responsibilities, even service in the armed forces. It is the very foundation of good citizenship. Today it is a principal instrument in awakening the child to cultural values, in preparing him for later professional training, and in helping him to adjust normally to his environment. In these days, it is doubtful that any child may reasonably be expected to succeed in life if he is denied the opportunity of an education. Such an opportunity, where the state has undertaken to provide it, is a right which must be made available to all on equal terms.

We come then to the question presented: Does segregation of children in public schools solely on the basis of race, even though the physical facilities and other "tangible" factors may be equal, deprive the children of the minority group of equal educational opportunities? We believe that it does.

In Sweatt v. Painter, supra, in finding that a segregated law school for Negroes could not provide them equal educational opportunities, this Court relied in large part on "those qualities which are incapable of objective measurement but which make for greatness in a law school." In McLaurin v. Oklahoma State Regents, supra, the Court, in requiring that a Negro admitted to a white graduate school be treated like all other students, again resorted to intangible considerations: ". . . his ability to study, to engage in discussions and exchange views with other students, and, in general, to learn his profession." Such considerations apply with added force to children in grade and high schools. To separate them from others of similar age and qualifications solely because of their race generates a feeling of inferiority as to their status in the community that may affect their hearts and minds in a way unlikely ever to be undone. The effect of this separation on their educational opportunities was well stated by a finding in the Kansas case by a court which nevertheless felt compelled to rule against the Negro plaintiffs:

> "Segregation of white and colored children in public schools has a detrimental effect upon the colored children. The impact is greater when it has the sanction of the law; for the policy of separating the races is usually interpreted as denoting the inferiority of the negro group. A sense of inferiority affects the motivation of a child to learn. Segregation with the sanction of law, therefore, has a tendency to [retard] the educational and mental development of negro children and to deprive them of some of the benefits they would receive in a racial[ly] integrated school system.[10]

Whatever may have been the extent of psychological knowledge at the time of Plessy v. Ferguson, this finding is amply supported by modern authority.[11] Any language in Plessy v. Ferguson contrary to this finding is rejected.

We conclude that in the field of public education the doctrine of "separate but equal" has no place. Separate educational facilities are inherently unequal. Therefore we hold that the plaintiffs and others similarly situated for whom the actions have been brought are, by reason of the segregation complained of, deprived of the equal protection of the laws guaranteed by the Fourteenth Amendment. This disposition makes unnecessary any discussion whether such segregation also violates the Due Process Clause of the Fourteenth Amendment.[12]

Because these are class actions, because of the wide applicability of this decision, and because of the great variety of local conditions, the formulation of decrees in these cases presents problems of considerable complexity. On reargument, the consideration of appropriate relief was necessarily subordinated to the primary question—the constitutionality of segregation in public education. We have now announced that such segregation is a denial of the equal protection of the laws. In order that we may have the full assistance of the parties in formulating decrees, the cases will be restored to the docket, and the parties are requested to present further argument on Questions 4 and 5 previously propounded by the Court for the reargument of this Term.[13] The Attorney General of the United States is again invited to participate. The Attorneys General of the states requiring or permitting segregation in public education will also be permitted to appear as amici curiae upon request to do so by September 15, 1954, and submission of briefs by October 1, 1954.[14]

Endnotes for Appendix C

*Briefs of amici curiae urging reversal were filed by Stephen J. Pollak, Ralph J. Moore, Jr., David Rubin, and Peter T. Galiano for the National Education Assn. et al.; by W. Reece Bader and James R. Madison for the San Francisco Lawyers' Committee for Urban Affairs; by J. Harold Flannery for the Center for Law and Education, Harvard University; by Herbert Teitelbaum for the Puerto Rican Legal Defense and Education Fund, Inc.; by Mario G. Obledo, Sanford J. Rosen, Michael Mendelson, and Alan Exelrod for the Mexican American Legal Defense and Educational Fund et al.; by Samuel Rabinove, Joseph B. Robison, Arnold Forster, and Elliot C. Rotherberg for the American Jewish Committee et al.; by F. Raymond Marks for the Childhood and Government Project; by Martin Glick for Efrain Tostado et al.; and by the Chinese Consolidated Benevolent Assn. et al.

1. A report adopted by the Human Rights Commission of San Francisco and submitted to the Court by respondents after oral argument shows that, as of April 1973, there were 3,457 Chinese students in the school system who spoke little or no English. The document further showed 2,136 students enrolled in Chinese special instruction classes, but at least 429 of the enrollees were not Chinese but were included for ethnic balance. Thus, as of April 1973, no more than 1,707 of the 3,457 Chinese students needing special English instruction were receiving it.

2. Section 602 provides:

    "Each Federal department and agency which is empowered to extend Federal financial assistance to any program or activity, by way of grant, loan, or contract other than a contract of insurance or guaranty, is authorized and directed to effectuate the provisions of section 2000d of this title with respect to such program or activity by issuing rules, regulations, or orders of general applicability which shall be consistent with achievement of the objectives of the statute authorizing the financial assistance in connection with which the action is taken..." 42 U.S.C. §2000d-1.

3. And see Report of the Human Rights Commission of San Francisco, Bilingual Education in the San Francisco Public Schools, Aug. 9, 1973.

4. 110 Cong. Rec. 6543 (Sen. Humphrey, quoting from President Kennedy's message to Congress, June 19, 1963).

5. These guidelines were issued in further clarification of the Department's position as stated in its regulations issued to implement Tit. VI, 45 CFR pt. 80. The regulations provide in part that no recipient of federal financial assistance administered by HEW may

"Provide any service, financial aid, or other benefit to an individual which is different, or is provided in a different manner, from that provided to others under the program; [or]

"Restrict an individual in any way in the enjoyment of any advantage or privilege enjoyed by others receiving any service, financial aid, or other benefit under the program."

45 CFR §80.3(b)(1)(ii), (iv).

6. The respondents do not contest the standing of the petitioners to sue as beneficiaries of the federal funding contract between the Department of Health, Education and Welfare and the San Francisco Unified School District.

7. Section 602, 42 U.S.C. §2000d-1, provides in pertinent part:

Each Federal department and agency which is empowered to extend Federal financial assistance to any program or activity, by way of grant, loan, or contract other than a contract of insurance or guaranty, is authorized and directed to effectuate the provisions of section 2000d of this title with respect to such program or activity by issuing rules, regulations, or orders of general applicability which shall be consistent with achievement of the objectives of the statute authorizing the financial assistance in connection with which the action is taken..."

The United States as amicus curiae asserts in its brief, and the respondents appear to concede, that the guidelines were issued pursuant to §602.

Endnotes for Appendix D

*Together with No. 2, Briggs et al. v. Elliott et al., on appeal from the United States District Court for the Eastern District of South Carolina, argued December 9-10, 1952, reargued December 7-8, 1953; No. 4, Davis et al. v. County School Board of Prince Edward County, Virginia, et al., on appeal from the United States District Court for the Eastern District of Virginia, argued December 10, 1952, reargued December 7-8, 1953; and No. 10, Gebhart et al. v. Belton et al., on certiorari to the Supreme Court of Delaware, argued December 11, 1952, reargued December 9, 1953.

1. In the Kansas case, Brown v. Board of Education, the plaintiffs are Negro children of elementary school age residing in Topeka. They brought this action in the United States District Court for the District of Kansas to enjoin enforcement of a Kansas statute which permits, but does not require, cities of more than 15,000 population to maintain separate school facilities for Negro and white students. Kan. Gen. Stat. §72-1724 (1949). Pursuant to that authority, the Topeka Board of Education elected to establish segregated

elementary schools. Other public schools in the community, however, are operated on a nonsegregated basis. The three-judge District Court, convened under 28 U.S.C. §§2281 and 2284, found that segregation in public education has a detrimental effect upon Negro children, but denied relief on the ground that the Negro and white schools were substantially equal with respect to buildings, transportation, curricula, and educational qualifications of teachers. 98 F. Supp. 797. The case is here on direct appeal under 28 U.S.C. §1253.

In the South Carolina case, Briggs v. Elliott, the plaintiffs are Negro children of both elementary and high school age residing in Clarendon County. They brought this action in the United States District Court for the Eastern District of South Carolina to enjoin enforcement of provisions in the state constitution and statutory code which require the segregation of Negroes and whites in public schools. S.C. Const., Art. XI, §7; S.C. Code §5377 (1942). The three-judge District Court, convened under 28 U.S.C. §§2281 and 2284, denied the requested relief. The court found that the Negro schools were inferior to the white schools and ordered the defendants to begin immediately to equalize the facilities. But the court sustained the validity of the contested provisions and denied the plaintiffs admission to the white schools during the equalization program. 98 F. Supp. 529. This Court vacated the District Court's judgment and remanded the case for the purpose of obtaining the court's views on a report filed by the defendants concerning the progress made in the equalization program. 342 U.S.s 350. On remand, the District Court found that substantial equality had been achieved except for buildings and that the defendants were proceeding to rectify this inequality as well. 103 F. Supp. 920. The case is again here on direct appeal under 28 U.S.C. §1253.

In the Virginia case, Davis v. County School Board, the plaintiffs are Negro children of high school age residing in Prince Edward County. They brought this action in the United States District Court for the Eastern District of Virginia to enjoin enforcement of provisions in the state constitution and statutory code which require the segregation of Negroes and whites in public schools. Va. Const., §140; Va. Code §22–221 (1950). The three-judge District Court, convened under 28 U.S.C. §§2281 and 2284, denied the requested relief. The court found the Negro school inferior in physical plant, curricula, and transportation, and ordered the defendants forthwith to provide substantially equal curricula and transportation and to "proceed with all reasonable diligence and dispatch to remove" the inequality in physical plant. But, as in the South Carolina case, the court sustained the validity of the contested provisions and denied the plaintiffs admission to the white schools during the equalization program. 103 F. Supp. 337. The case is here on direct appeal under 28 U.S.C. §1253.

In the Delaware case, Gebhart v. Belton, the plaintiffs are Negro children of both elementary and high school age residing in New Castle County. They brought this action in the Delaware Court of Chancery to enjoin enforcement of provisions in the state constitution and statutory code which require the segregation of Negroes and whites in public schools. Del. Const., Art. X, §2; Del. Rev. Code §2631 (1935). The Chancellor gave judgment for the plaintiffs and ordered their immediate admission to schools previously attended only by white children, on the ground that the Negro schools were inferior with respect to teacher training, pupil-teacher ratio, extracurricular activities, physical plant, and time and distance involved in travel. 87 A.2d 862. The Chancellor also found that segregation itself results in an inferior education for Negro children (see note 10, infra), but did not rest his decision on that ground. Id., at 865. The Chancellor's decree was affirmed by the Supreme Court of Delaware, which intimated, however, that the defendants might be able to obtain a modification of the decree after equalization of the Negro and white schools had been accomplished. 91 A.2d 137, 152. The defendants, contending only that the Delaware courts had erred in ordering the immediate admission of the Negro plaintiffs to the white schools, applied to this Court for certiorari. The writ was granted, 344 U.S. 891. The plaintiffs, who were successful below, did not submit a cross-petition.

2. 344 U.S. 1, 141, 891.

3. 345 U.S. 972. The Attorney General of the United States participated both Terms as amicus curiae.

4. For a general study of the development of public education prior to the Amendment, see Butts and Cremin, A History of Education in American Culture (1953), Pts. I, II; Cubberley, Public Education in the United States 91934 ed.), cc. II–XII. School practices current at the time of the adoption of the Fourteenth Amendment are described in Butts and Cremin, supra, at 269–275; Cubberley, supra, at 288–339, 408–431; Knight, Public Education in the South (1922), cc. VIII, IX. See also H. Ex. Doc. No. 315, 41st Cong., 2d Sess. (1871). Although the demand for free public schools followed substantially the same pattern in both the North and the South, the development in the South did not begin to gain momentum until about 1850, some twenty years after that in the North. The reasons for the somewhat slower development in the South (e.g., the rural character of the South and the different regional attitudes toward state assistance) are well explained in Cubberley, supra, at 408–423. In the country as a whole, but particularly in the South, the War virtually stopped all progress in public education. Id., at 427–428. The low status of Negro education in all sections of the country, both before and immediately after the War, is described in Beale, a History of Freedom of Teaching in American Schools (1941), 112–132, 175–195. Compulsory school attendance laws were not generally adopted until after the ratification of the Fourteenth Amendment, and it was not until 1918 that such laws were in force in all the states. Cubberley, supra, at 563–565.

5. Slaughter-House Cases, 16 Wall. 36, 67–72 (1873); Strauder v. West Virginia, 100 U.S. 303, 307–308 (1880):

    "It ordains that no State shall deprive any person of life, liberty, or property, without due process of law, or deny to any person within its jurisdiction the equal protection of the laws. What is this but declaring that the law in the States shall be the same for the black as for the white; that all persons, whether colored or white, shall stand equal before the laws of the States, and, in regard to the colored race, for whose protection the amendment was primarily designed, that no discrimination shall be made against them by law because of their color? The words of the amendment, it is true, are prohibitory, but they contain a necessary implication of a positive immunity, or right, most valuable to the colored race,—the right to exemption from unfriendly legislation against them distinctively as colored,— exemption from legal discriminations, implying inferiority in civil society, lessening the security of their enjoyment of the rights which others enjoy, and discriminations which are steps toward reducing them; to the condition of a subject race."

6. The doctrine apparently originated in Roberts v. City of Boston, 59 Mass. 198, 206 (1850), upholding school segregation against attack as being violative of a state constitutional guarantee of equality. Segregation in Boston public schools was eliminated in 1855. Mass. Acts 1855, c. 256. But elsewhere in the North segregation in public education has persisted in some communities until recent years. It is apparent that such segregation has long been a nationwide problem, not merely one of sectional concern.

7. See also Berea College v. Kentucky, 211 U.S. 45 (1908).

8. In the Cumming case, Negro taxpayers sought an injunction requiring the defendant school board to discontinue the operation of a high school for white children until the board resumed operation of a high school for Negro children. Similarly, in the Gong Lum case, the plaintiff, a child of Chinese descent, contended only that state authorities had misapplied the doctrine by classifying him with Negro children and requiring him to attend a Negro school.

9. In the Kansas case, the court below found substantial equality as to all such factors. 98 F. Supp. 797, 798. In the South Carolina case, the court below found that the defendants were proceeding "promptly and in good faith to comply with the court's decree." 103 F. Supp. 920, 921. In the Virginia case, the court below noted that the equalization program was already "afoot and progressing." (103 F. Supp. 337, 341). Since then, we have been advised, in the Virginia Attorney General's brief on reargument, that the program has now been completed. In the Delaware case, the court below similarly noted that the state's equalization program was well under way. 91 A.2d 137, 149.

10. A similar finding was made in the Delaware case: "I conclude from the testimony that in our Delaware society, State-imposed segregation in education itself results in the Negro children, as a class, receiving educational opportunities which are substantially inferior to those available to white children otherwise similarly situated." 87 A.2d 862, 865.

11. K.B. Clark, Effect of Prejudice and Discrimination on Personality Development (Midcentury White House Conference on Children and Youth, 1950); Witmer and Kotinsky, Personality in the Making (1952), c. VI; Deutscher and Chein, The Psychological Effects of Enforced Segregation: A Survey of Social Science Opinion, 26 J. Psychol. 259 (1948); Chein, What are the Psychological Effects of Segregation Under Conditions of Equal Facilities?, 3 Int. J. Opinion and Attitude Res. 229 (1949); Brameld Educational Costs, in Discrimination and National Welfare (MacIver, ed., 1949), 44–48; Frazier, The Negro in the United States (1949), 674–681. And see generally Myrdal, An American Dilemma (1944).

12. See Bolling v. Sharpe, post, p. 497, concerning the Due Process Clause of the Fifth Amendment.

13. "4. Assuming it is decided that segregation in public schools violates the Fourteenth Amendment.

"(a) would a decree necessarily follow providing that, within the limits set by normal geographic school distracting, Negro children should forthwith be admitted to schools of their choice, or

"(b) may this Court, in the exercise of its equity powers, permit an effective gradual adjustment to be brought about from existing segregated systems to a system not based on color distinctions?

"5. On the assumption on which questions 4(a) and (b) are based, and assuming further that this Court will exercise its equity powers to the end described in question 4(b), "(a) should this Court formulate detailed decrees in these cases;

"(b) if so, what specific issues should the decrees reach;

"(c) should this Court appoint a special master to hear evidence with a view to recommending specific terms for such decrees;

"(d) should this Court remand to the courts of first instance with directions to frame decrees in these cases, and if so what general directions should the decrees of this Court include and what procedures should the courts of first instance follow in arriving at the specific terms of more detailed decrees?"

14. See Rule 42, Revised Rules of this Court (effective July 1, 1954).

Bibliography

Books

Almond, Gabriel and Powell, Jr., G. Bingham. 1966. *Comparative Politics: A Developmental Approach*. Boston: Little Brown and Company.

Bachrach, Peter. 1966. *The Theory of Democratic Elitism: A Critique*. Boston: Little Brown and Company.

Berman, Ronald. 1968. *America in the Sixties*. New York: Free Press.

Boulding, Kenneth E. 1956. *The Image*. Quoted in Malcolm E. Jewell and Samuel C. Patterson. *The Legislative Process of the United States*. New York: Random House.

Burns, MacGregor. 1963. *The Deadlock of Democracy*. New Jersey: Prentice-Hall, Inc.

Carnegie Corporation. 1979. *Annual Report*. New York: Carnegie Corporation.

Center for Applied Linguistics (CAL). 1977. *Bilingual Education: Current Perspectives-Law*. Arlington, VA: CAL.

Chilcote, Ronald H. 1981. *Theories of Comparative Politics: The Search for A Paradigm*. Boulder, Colorado: Westview Press.

Clapp, Charles L. 1964. *The Congressman: His Work as He Sees It*. Washington, DC: The Brooking Institution.

Coser, Lewis. 1956. *The Functions of Social Conflict*. New York: Free Press.

Crotty, William J. and Garry C. Jacobson. 1980. *American Parties in Decline*. Boston: Little Brown and Company.

Danoff, Malcolm N. et. al. 1978. *Evaluation of the Impact of ESEA Title VII Spanish/English Bilingual Education Program*. 3 vols. Palo Alto, CA: American Institutes for Research.

Dye, Thomas R. and Harman L Zeigler. 1975. *The Irony of Democracy: An Uncommon Introduction to American Politics*. Belmont, California: Wadsworth Publishing Company.

Easton, David. 1953. *The Political System.* New York: Knopf.

Easton, David. 1965a. *A Framework for Political Analysis.* Englewood Cliffs, NJ: Prentice-Hall.

Easton, David. 1965b. *A Systems Analysis of Political Life.* New York: John Wiley and Sons.

Easton, David, Eugene Eidenberg, and Roy Morey. 1969. *An Act of Congress.* New York: W.W. Norton & Co., Inc.

Eldenberg, Eugene and Roy D. Morey. 1969. *Act of Congress.* New York, NY: W.W. Nortin.

Epstein, Noel. 1977. *Language, Ethnicity and the Schools.* Washington, DC: Institute for Education Leadership.

Fiorina, Morris P. 1977. *Congress: Keystone of the Washington Establishment.* New Haven and London: Yale University Press.

Galbraith, John Kenneth. 1976. *The Affluent Society.* New York: Houghton Mifflin Company.

Garcia, F. Chris. ed. 1974. *La Causa Politica: A Chicano Politics Reader.* Notre Dame, IN: University of Notre Dame Press.

Hakuta, Kenji. 1986. *Mirror of Language.* New York: Basic Books.

Harrington, Michael. 1963. *The Other America: Poverty in the United States.* New York: The Macmillan Company.

Ingram, Hellen M. and Dean F. Mann. eds. 1980. *Why Policies Succeed or Fail.* Beverly Hills, CA: Sage Publications.

Jewell, Malcolm E. and Samuel C. Patterson. 1966. *The Legislative Process of the United States.* New York: Random House.

Jones, Charles O. 1984. *An Introduction to the Study of Public Policy.* Belmont, California: Brooks/Cole.

Kloss, H. 1977. *The American Bilingual Tradition.* Rowley, MA: Newbury House.

Ladd, Everett C. 1970. *American Political Parties.* New York: W. W. Norton Company.

Lasswell, Harold. 1936. *Politics: Who Gets What, When and How.* New York: Meridian Books.

Leuchtenburg, William E. 1973. *A Troubled Feast: American Society Since 1945.* Boston: Little Brown and Company.

Lillibridge, G. D. 1976. *Images of American Society.* Boston: Houghton Mifflin Company.

Mackey, William F. and V. N. Beebe. 1977. *Bilingual Schools for a Bicultural Community.* Rowley, MA: Newbury House.

Mayhew, David R. 1975. *Congress: The Electoral Connection*. New Haven, Connecticut: Yale University Press.

Miles, Matthew B. and A. Michael Huberman. 1984. *Qualitative Data Analysis*. Beverly Hills: Sage Publications.

Mills, C. Wright. 1956. *The Power Elite*. New York: Oxford University Press.

Morgenthau, Hans J. 1958. *Dilemmas of Politics*. Chicago: University of Chicago Press.

NACBE. 1979. *Fourth Annual Report on the NACBE*. Washington, DC: NACBE.

Okeefe, William J. and Morris S. Ogul. 1977. *The American Legislative Process, Congress and the States*. Englewood Cliffs, New Jersey: Prentice Hall, Inc.

Oleszek, Walter. 1978. *Congressional Procedures and the Policy Process*. Washington, DC: Congressional Quarterly Press.

O'Malley, James M. 1982. *Children's English and Services Study: Educational and Needs Assessment for Language Minority Children with Limited English Proficiency*. Rosslyn, VA: InterAmerica Research Associates.

Ornstein, Norman J. and Shirley Elder. 1978. *Interest Group, Lobbying and Policy Making*. Washington, DC: Congressional Quarterly Press.

Parenti, Michael. 1983. *Democracy for the Few*. New York: St. Martins Press, Inc.

Patterson, James T. 1976. *America in the Twentieth Century*. New York: Harcourt Brace Jovanovich, Inc.

Paulston, Christina B. 1980. *Bilingual Education: Theories and Issues*. Rowley, MA: Newbury House.

Rieselbach, Leroy N. 1970. *The Congressional System: Notes and Readings*. Belmont, CA: Duxbury Press.

Ripley, Randall B. and Grace A. Franklin. 1987. *Congress, The Bureaucracy and Public Policy*. Chicago, Illinois: The Dorsey Press.

Rourke, Francis E. 1976. *Bureaucracy, Politics and Public Policy*. Boston: Little Brown and Company.

Scarrow, Howard A. 1969. *Comparative Political Analysis: An Introduction*. New York: Harper and Row.

Schattschneider, E. E. 1960. *The Semisovereign People*. New York: Holt, Reinhart and Winston.

Todd, Paul L. and Merle Curti. 1977. *Rise of the American Nation*. New York: Harcourt Brace Jovanovich, Inc.

Wade, Larry. 1972. *The Elements of Public Policy*. Columbus, Ohio: Charles E. Merrill.

Wilson, Woodrow. 1956. *Congressional Government.* New York: Meridian Books.

Woytinsky, Emma S. 1967. *Profile of the US Economy.* New York: Praeger Publishers.

Young, Oran. 1968. *Systems of Political Science.* Englewood Cliffs, NJ: Prentice-Hall.

Articles

Almond, Gabriel A. 1960. Introduction: A Functional Approach to Comparative Politics. In *The Politics of Developing Areas.* Edited by Gabriel A. Almond and James S. Coleman. Princeton: University Press.

Almond, Gabriel A. 1969–1970. Determinacy-Choice, Stability-Change: Some Thoughts on a Contemporary Polemic in Political Theory. *Government and Opposition* (vol. 4:22–40).

American Institute for Research (AIR). 1977–1978. Evaluation of the Impact of ASEA Title VII Spanish/English Bilingual Education Program.

American Institute of Public Opinion. November 5, 1965. Release.

Birman, Beatrice F. and Allen L. Ginsburg. 1983. Introduction: Addressing the Needs of Language-Minority Children. In *Bilingual Education of Federal Policy.* Edited by K. A. de Kanter. Lexington, MA: Lexington Books.

Blanco, Gustavo. 1978. The Implementation of Bilingual/Bicultural Education Programs in the United States. In *Case Studies in Bilingual Education.* Edited by B. Spolsky and R. Cooper. Rowley, MA: Newbury House.

Center for Applied Linguistics. 1980. CAL Offers Comments on Proposed Law Regulations. *The Linguistic Reporter* (vol. 23, no.3).

Crawford, James. 1984. Bilingual Education: Language Learning and Politics. *Education Week* (April).

Department of Education. 1990. Nondiscrimination Under Programs Receiving Federal Assistance Through the Education Department. *Federal Registrar.* Washington, DC: Government Printing Office.

Easton, David. 1957. An Approach to the Analysis of Political Systems. *World Politics* (April).

Elegoet, Fanch. 1973. Bilingisme ou domination linguistique? *Les Temps Moderns* (nos. 324, 325, 326).

Fenno, Jr., Richard F. 1962. The House Appropriations Committee as a

Political System: The Problem of Integration. *American Political Science Review* (vol. 56:310-324).

Finer, Samuel E. 1969-1970. Almond's Concept of 'The Political System': A Textual Critique. *Government and Opposition* (vol. 4:3-21).

Fishman, Joshua A. 1980. Speech at Georgetown University Roundtable. Washington, DC: March 21.

Gross, Bertram M. 1967. A Systems Analysis of Political Life (a Review). *The American Political Science Review* (vol. 61:157).

Guadalupe, Jr., SanMiguel. 1983. In the Background: Conflict and Controversy in the Evolution of Bilingual Education Legislation in Texas 1965-73. *NABE Journal* (vol. 7, no. 3).

Haugen, E. 1972. The Stigmata of Bilingualism. In *The Ecology of Language-Essays* by Einar Haugen. Edited by A. S. Dil. Stanford, CA: Stanford University Press.

Judd, Elliot L. 1977. Factors Affecting the Passage of the Bilingual Education Act of 1967 (Unpublished Ph.D. Dissertation, New York University).

Kaplan, Morton. 1967. Systems Theory. In *Contemporary Political Analysis*. Edited by J. C. Charlesworth. New York: John Wiley and Sons.

Klonoski, James R. 1967. A Systems Analysis in Political Life (a Review). *The Western Political Quarterly* (vol. 20:738).

Lambert, Wallace E. 1978. Some Cognitive and Sociocultural Consequences of Being Bilingual. In *International Dimensions of Bilingual Education*. Edited by J. E. Alatis. Washington, DC: Georgetown University Press.

Leibowitz, Arnold H. 1980. The Bilingual Education Act: A Legislative Analysis (a NACBE Report).

Lieberson, Stanley. 1981. Bilingualism in Montreal: A Demographic Analysis. In *Language Diversity and Language Contact*. Edited by A. S. Dil. Stanford, CA: Stanford University Press.

McClonsky, Herbert, Paul Hoffman, and Rosemary Ottaro. 1963. Issues, Conflict and Consensus Among Party Leaders and Followers. *American Political Science Review* (vol. lvii).

Miller, Eugene F. 1971. David Easton's Political Theory. *Political Science Review* (vol. 1).

Moran, Rachel F. 1988. The Politics of Discretion: Intervention in Bilingual Education. *California Law Review* (vol. 76).

Paulston, Christina B. 1974. Implications of Language Learning Theory for Language Planning: Concerns in Bilingual Education. In *Papers in Applied Linguistics*. Arlington, VA: Center for Applied Linguistics.

Pennock, Roland. 1962. Democracy and Leadership. In *Democracy Today.* Edited by William Chambers and Robert Salisbury. New York: Macmillan Company.

Reading, Reid R. 1972. Is Easton's System-Persistence Framework Useful? A Research Note. In *Journal of Politics* (vol. 34:258-267).

Spiro, Herbert. 1967. An Evaluation of Systems Theory. In *Contemporary Political Analysis.* Edited by J.C. Charlesworth. New York: Free Press.

Spiro, Herbert. 1981. Hispanics Make Their Move. In *US News and World Report* (August 24:60-64).

Stoller, Peter. 1976. The Language Planning Activities of the US Office of Bilingual Education. In *International Journal of the Sociology of Language* (vol.11).

Teitelbaum, Herbert and Richard J. Hiller. 1977. The Legal Perspective. In *Bilingual Education: Current Perspectives vol. 3.* Arlington, VA: Center for Applied Linguistics.

Government Documents

Alexander, Herbert. 1982. *United States Senate Congressional Record* (Statement to the United States Senate on January 26).

Ford, Gerald R. 1967. *United States Congressional Record, Vol. 133, 90th Congress, 1st session: House Hearings on H.R. 7819 ESEA Amendments.* Washington, DC: Government Printing Office.

Johnson, Lyndon B. 1965. *United States Congressional Record, President's Address to a Joint Session of Congress on January 4, 1965.* Washington, DC: Government Printing Office.

United States Bureau of the Census. *1960 Census Report.* Washington, DC: Government Printing Office.

United States Commission on Civil Rights. 1975. *A Better Chance to Learn: Bilingual Bicultural Education.* Washington, DC: Government Printing Office.

United States Congress. 1969. *Congress and the Nation, Vol. II.* Washington, DC: Congressional Service Quarterly.

United States Congress. 1965. *Congressional Record, Vol. III, Pt. 21, 89th Congress, 1st Session* (October 27). Washington, DC: Government Printing Office.

United States Congress. 1967. *Hearings Before the Senate Special Committee on*

Bilingual Education of the Committee of Labor and Public Welfare, 90th Congress, 1st Session: 75. Washington, DC: Government Printing Office.

United States Congress. 1967. *H.R. Document 272, 90th Congress, 2nd Session: 5.* Washington, DC: Government Printing Office.

United States Congress. 1969. *Senate Special Subcommittee on Indian Education of the Committee of Labor and Public Welfare, 91st Congress, 1st Session: 19.* Washington, DC: Government Printing Office.

United States Congress. 1975. *Hearings Before the Senate Special Committee on Bilingual Education of the Committee of Labor and Public Welfare, 94th Congress, 1st Session.* Washington, DC: Government Printing Office.

United States Congress. 1977. *Bilingual Education: Hearings on H.R. 15 Before the Subcommittee on Elementary, Secondary, and Vocational Education of the House Committee on Education and Labor, 95th Congress, 1st Session, iii-iv.* Washington, DC: Government Printing Office.

United States Congress. 1977. *House of Representatives Report No. 1137, 95th Congress, 2nd Session.* Washington, DC: Government Printing Office.

United States Congress. 1970. *Bilingual Education Act of 1978, Public Law No. 95-561, Section 703, 93 Stat. 2268, 2270* (later codified as amended at 20 United States Congress Section 3223, 1982 and Supplement IV, 1986). Washington, DC: Government Printing Office.

United States Congress. 1978. *Oversight Hearing on the Educational Literacy and Social Needs of the Hispanic Community: Hearing Before the House Committee on Education and Labor, 100th Congress, Session 1.* Washington, DC: Government Printing Office.

United States Congress. 1982. *Bilingual Education Amendments of 1981: Hearings on S. 2002 Before the Subcommittee on Education, Arts and Humanities of the Senate Committee on Labor and Human Resources, 97th Congress, 2nd Session, iii-v.* Washington, DC: Government Printing Office.

United States Congress. 1983. *The Bilingual Education Improvement Act of 1983: Hearings on H.R. 2682 Before the Subcommittee on Elementary, Secondary, and Vocational Education of the House Committee on Education and Labor, 98th Congress, 1st Session.* Washington, DC: Government Printing Office.

United States Congress. 1984. *Bilingual Education: Hearings on H.R. 11 and H.R. 5231 Before the Subcommittee on Elementary, Secondary, and Vocational Education of the House Committee on Education and Labor, 98th Congress, 2nd Session, iii.* Washington, DC: Government Printing Office.

Interviews

Anonymous respondents

Cubillios, Ernest. United States English, Washington, DC, 20 August, 1992.

Gomez, Juan. National Clearinghouse for Bilingual Education, Washington, DC, 15 June, 1992.

Lyons, Jim. National Association for Bilingual Education, Washington, DC, 23 October, 1992.

Nichol, Francis. District of Columbia Public Schools, Washington, DC, 29 July, 1992.

Index

About the Authors

ABDUL KARIM BANGURA is Researcher-In-Residence at the Center for Global Peace and Assistant Professor of International Relations in the School of International Service at American University, and the Director of The African Institution. He received his Gdpl. in the Social Sciences from Stockholms Universitet in Sweden, Ph.D. in Political Science from Howard University, Ph.D. in Development Economics from the University of Maryland Baltimore Graduate School, and Ph.D. in Linguistics from Georgetown University.

MARTIN CHUKS MUO is a Research Associate at The African Institution and teaches in the District of Columbia Public Schools System, Washington, DC. He holds a Ph.D. in Political Science from Howard University.